KEBAB IT !

KEBAB IT!

It seems to me that shish kebabs have been getting the short end of the stick because the rare time you do come across a kebab dinner is usually in a restaurant and with only a selection of two on the menu! Now don't you agree that it would be far more interesting (and less expensive) to experience the delight of scallop kebabs nestled on a bed of fried parsley? I thought you would and that is the reason for this book which is just brimming with innovative and exciting kebab recipes for the home. For those of you who have yet to make kebabs before, be assured that it is easy and little effort is needed for success especially if you have these utensils: a selection of skewers in metal and wood, a large ovenproof platter and a very sharp knife for accurate trimming and shaping. I urge you to be creative with these recipes and by all means serve them for lunch as well as dinner. Besides fantastic meat and fish kebabs you will find some super vegetable kebabs that are ideal for spicing up an otherwise routine meal and a selection of fun desserts that can add the finishing touch. So with your skewers in hand, off we go to the kitchen — let's prepare something different tonight!

Mustard Marinade for Meat or Fish

1 SERVING	207 CALORIES	0g CARBOHYDRATE
0g PROTEIN	23g FAT	0g FIBER

1¼ cups	(300 ml) olive oil
5 tbsp	(75 ml) Dijon mustard
2	garlic cloves, smashed and chopped
1 tsp	(5 ml) tarragon
	juice 1 lemon
	few drops Tabasco sauce
	salt and pepper

Mix all ingredients together in small bowl. Pour marinade over chosen meat or fish and refrigerate 30 minutes.

In preparation for cooking, drain marinade and reserve for basting.

This marinade is strong enough to use just as flavouring without marinating 30 minutes. Keep this in mind if you are short of time.

Marinade for Lamb or Fish

1 SERVING	175 CALORIES	1g CARBOHYDRATE
0g PROTEIN	19g FAT	0g FIBER

1 cup	(250 ml) olive oil
3	garlic cloves, smashed and chopped
3	shallots, finely chopped
½ cup	(125 ml) lemon juice
½ tsp	(2 ml) crushed rosemary
½ tsp	(2 ml) oregano
	salt and pepper

Mix all ingredients together in small bowl. Pour marinade over chosen lamb or fish and refrigerate overnight.

In preparation for cooking, drain marinade and reserve for basting.

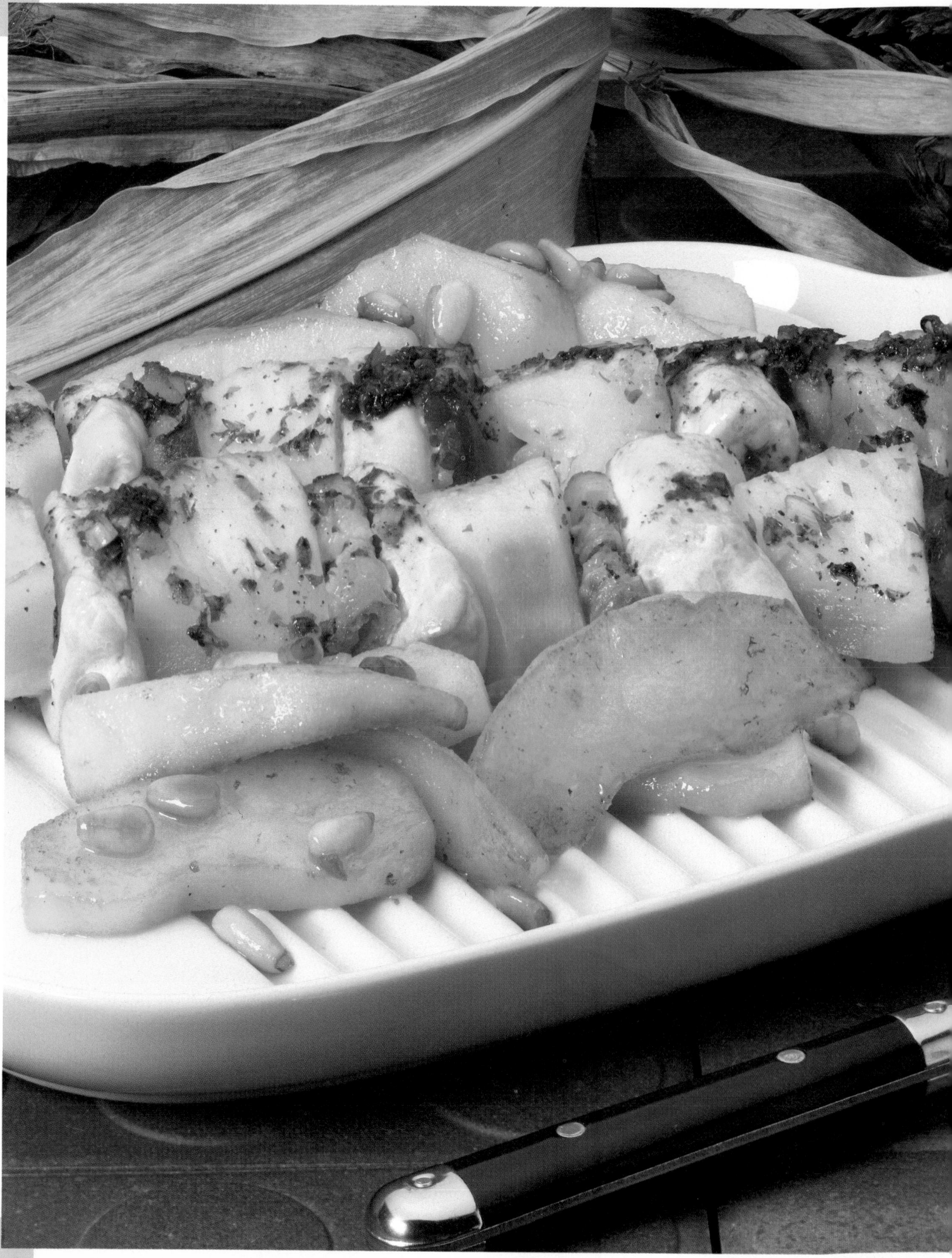

Pineapple Chicken Kebabs

(serves 4)

1 SERVING	321 CALORIES	12g CARBOHYDRATE
21g PROTEIN	21g FAT	0.4g FIBER

2	chicken breasts, skinned, halved and boned
½	pineapple, cut in 1 in (2.5 cm) pieces
5	slices cooked bacon, cut in half
3 tbsp	(45 ml) butter
2	garlic cloves, smashed and chopped
2 tbsp	(30 ml) chopped parsley
	few drops Worcestershire sauce
	salt and pepper

Preheat oven to 450°F (240°C).

Cut chicken in 1 in (2.5 cm) pieces. Alternate along with pineapple and bacon on skewers; set aside.

Melt butter in small saucepan over medium heat. Stir in garlic, parsley and Worcestershire sauce.

Set skewers on ovenproof platter and baste with melted butter mixture. Season well with pepper.

Cook 12 minutes in oven, turning skewers over once or twice. Baste again if desired.

These kebabs serve well with sautéed apples and pine nuts.

The first step in making kebabs is to prepare the ingredients as directed in the recipe.

A simple mixture of butter, garlic, parsley and Worcestershire sauce will give a delicious flavour to kebabs.

Alternate chicken, pineapple and bacon on skewers.

It is important to baste the ingredients evenly before cooking.

Marinated Drumsticks

(serves 4)

1 SERVING	277 CALORIES	13g CARBOHYDRATE
27g PROTEIN	13g FAT	1.4g FIBER

2 lb	(900 g) chicken drumsticks
1 tbsp	(15 ml) Trinidad-style hot sauce
1 tsp	(5 ml) Worcestershire sauce
2 tbsp	(30 ml) oil
1	green pepper, in bite-size pieces
2	bananas (not too ripe) peeled and sliced thick
	salt and pepper

Preheat oven to 450°F (240°C).

Score drumsticks with knife and place in plate.

Sprinkle hot sauce, Worcestershire, oil, salt and pepper over chicken.

Place chicken on skewers and cook 10 minutes in oven. Turn skewers over and cook another 10 minutes.

Remove drumsticks from skewers and let cool.

Alternate chicken, green pepper and banana on skewers; place on ovenproof platter. Cook 8 minutes in oven.

Serve with a spicy sauce.

Score drumsticks with knife and place on plate. **1**

Place chicken on skewers and cook 20 minutes in oven. **3**

Sprinkle hot sauce, Worcestershire, oil, salt and pepper over chicken. **2**

Add green pepper and banana to skewers with chicken; finish cooking 8 minutes. **4**

Indonesian Chicken

(serves 4)

1 SERVING	381 CALORIES	7g CARBOHYDRATE
23g PROTEIN	29g FAT	1.0g FIBER

2	chicken breasts, skinned, halved and boned
½ cup	(125 ml) chopped walnuts
½ cup	(125 ml) lime juice
1 cup	(250 ml) hot chicken stock
2	garlic cloves, smashed and chopped
1 tbsp	(15 ml) olive oil
1 cup	(250 ml) sour cream
2 tbsp	(30 ml) chopped chives
	salt and pepper

Cut chicken into ½ in (1.2 cm) pieces. Place in bowl along with walnuts, lime juice, chicken stock, garlic, salt and pepper; marinate 2 hours in refrigerator.

Thread chicken on skewers and place on ovenproof platter. Reserve ⅓ of marinade.

Baste skewers with oil and broil 6 to 7 minutes each side in oven 6 in (15 cm) from top element.

Before kebabs are done, mix reserved marinade with sour cream and chives. Serve with chicken.

Spicy Chicken Breasts

(serves 4)

1 SERVING	290 CALORIES	23g CARBOHYDRATE
27g PROTEIN	10g FAT	1.2g FIBER

¾ lb	(375 g) mushroom caps, cleaned
¼ tsp	(1 ml) lemon juice
1 lb	(500 g) chicken breasts, skinned, halved and boned
1 tbsp	(15 ml) Worcestershire sauce
2	beaten eggs
1 cup	(250 ml) breadcrumbs
1	red pepper, in bite-size pieces
	Mexican hot sauce to taste
	few drops melted butter

Preheat oven to 450°F (240°C).

Place mushroom caps in bowl and sprinkle with lemon juice; set aside.

Cut chicken in 1 in (2.5 cm) pieces and place in another bowl; add Worcestershire sauce and hot sauce. Marinate 15 minutes on countertop.

Pour beaten eggs into large bowl. Using tongs add chicken pieces; mix until coated.

Roll chicken in breadcrumbs and alternate along with mushroom caps and red pepper on skewers.

Place skewers on ovenproof platter and sprinkle with melted butter. Cook 15 minutes in oven, turning skewers over once or twice.

Marinate chicken pieces in Worcestershire and hot sauces. Place bowl on counter for 15 minutes.

Roll chicken in breadcrumbs.

Coat marinated chicken in beaten eggs.

Alternate chicken, mushroom caps and red pepper on skewers.

Garlic Wing Kebabs

(serves 4)

1 SERVING	251 CALORIES	14g CARBOHYDRATE
15g PROTEIN	15g FAT	0.9g FIBER

32	chicken wings, middle section only
3	garlic cloves, smashed and chopped
½ cup	(125 ml) barbecue sauce
2 tbsp	(30 ml) honey
1 tbsp	(15 ml) lemon juice
2 tbsp	(30 ml) oil
1 tbsp	(15 ml) wine vinegar
½ tsp	(2 ml) brown sugar
16	green onion sticks, 1½ in (4 cm) long
16	zucchini sticks, 1½ in (4 cm) long
	salt and pepper

Place wings, garlic, barbecue sauce, honey, lemon juice, oil, vinegar and brown sugar in bowl; marinate 30 minutes in refrigerator.

Drain and reserve marinade.

Alternate onion, chicken and zucchini on skewers; place in ovenproof dish. Baste with marinade and season well. Broil 12 minutes 6 in (15 cm) from top element; turn over twice.

Change oven setting to 450°F (240°C) and finish cooking 7 minutes close to bottom of oven. Season during cooking.

Serve kebabs in baskets if available.

Note that the middle section of the wings should be used for the kebabs. Use remaining wing parts for other recipes.

Marinate wings in garlic, barbecue sauce, honey, lemon juice, oil, vinegar and brown sugar.

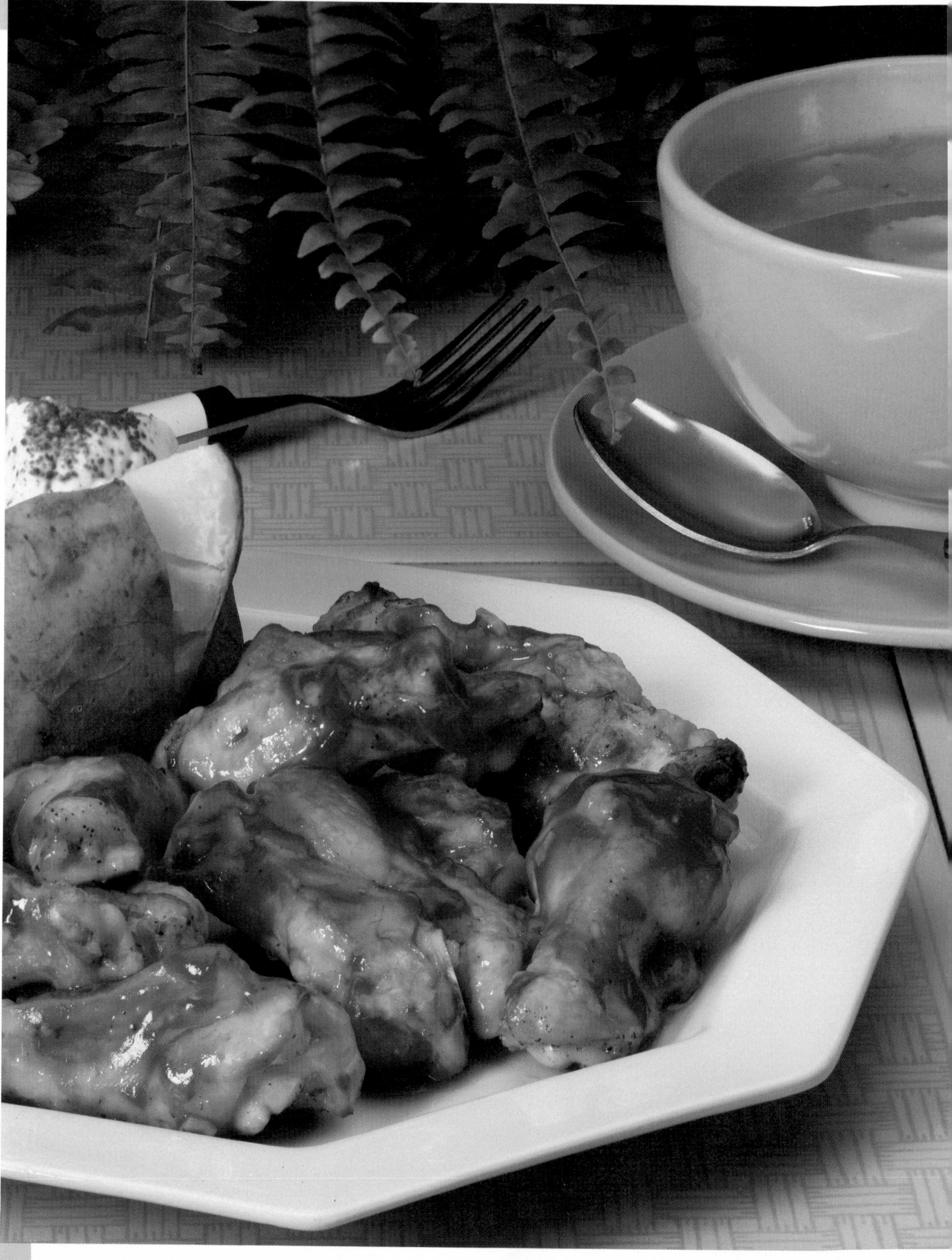

Mid-Wing Skewers

(serves 4)

1 SERVING	153 CALORIES	4g CARBOHYDRATE
14g PROTEIN	9g FAT	0g FIBER

32	chicken wings, middle section only
12 oz	(355 ml) can beer
2	green onions, thinly sliced
½ cup	(125 ml) catsup
2 tbsp	(30 ml) HP sauce
1 tbsp	(15 ml) soya sauce
1 tbsp	(15 ml) finely chopped fresh ginger
1 tbsp	(15 ml) wine vinegar
¼ tsp	(1 ml) Tabasco sauce
1 tbsp	(15 ml) honey
1 tbsp	(15 ml) oil
	salt and pepper

Preheat oven to 450°F (240°C).

Reserve leftover parts of wings for other recipes. Place the middle sections in bowl; add beer and green onions. Marinate 1 hour in refrigerator.

Meanwhile, mix catsup, HP sauce, soya sauce, ginger, vinegar, Tabasco and honey together; set aside.

Drain chicken and discard marinade. Fill skewers with chicken and place in ovenproof dish; season well and baste with oil.

Cook skewers 18 minutes in middle of oven; turn over twice.

Remove from oven and baste with catsup mixture. Change oven setting to Grill (Broil) and place dish on rack 4 in (10 cm) from top element; broil 5 to 6 minutes.

Turn skewers over, baste again and finish broiling 5 to 6 minutes.

Remove chicken from skewers and accompany with baked potatoes.

Marinate chicken in beer and onions for 1 hour in refrigerator.

Mix catsup, HP sauce, soya sauce, ginger, vinegar, Tabasco and honey together; set aside. This mixture will give chicken lots of flavour.

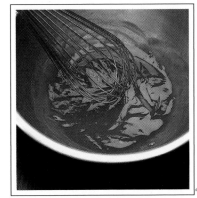

Chicken, Onions and Zucchini

(serves 4)

1 SERVING	166 CALORIES	8g CARBOHYDRATE
20g PROTEIN	6g FAT	1.4g FIBER

1 lb	(500 g) chicken breasts, skinned, halved and boned
1 tbsp	(15 ml) chopped fresh ginger
3 tbsp	(45 ml) soya sauce
1	garlic clove, smashed and chopped
8	pearl onions, blanched
1	yellow pepper, in bite-size pieces
8	small pieces zucchini
1	red pepper, in bite-size pieces
4	lemon wedges
1 tbsp	(15 ml) oil
	salt and pepper

Cut chicken into ½ in (1.2 cm) cubes. Place in bowl along with ginger, soya sauce and garlic; marinate 30 minutes in refrigerator.

Drain chicken and reserve marinade.

Alternate chicken, vegetables and lemon wedges on skewers. Place in ovenproof dish and season well. Baste with marinade and sprinkle with oil.

Broil 8 minutes in oven 6 in (15 cm) from top element. Turn skewers over once and baste with marinade twice.

Marinate chicken in ginger, soya sauce and garlic for 30 minutes in refrigerator.

Alternate chicken, vegetables and lemon wedges on skewers. The lemon will give a special flavour.

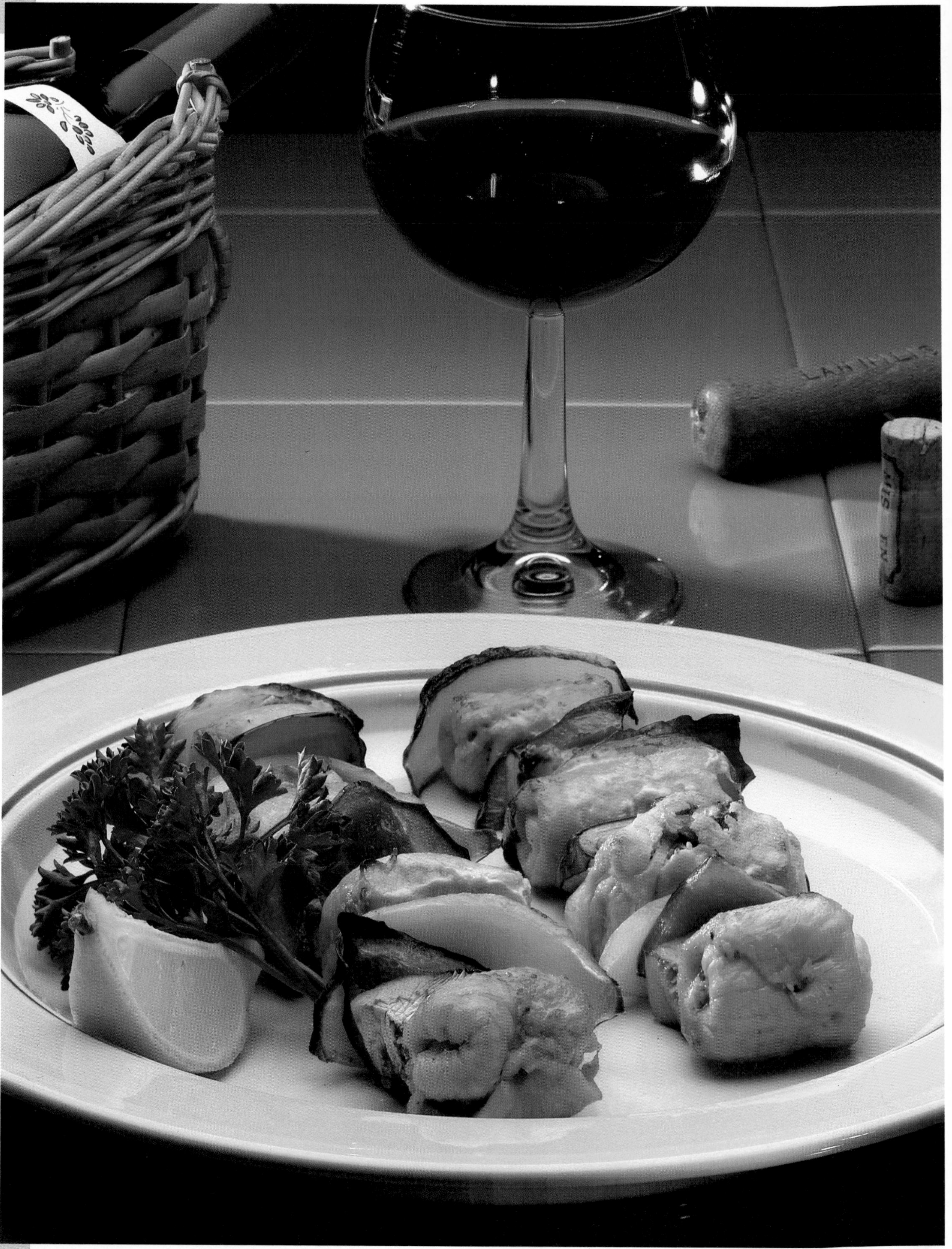

Stuffed Turkey on Skewers

(serves 4)

1 SERVING	321 CALORIES	4g CARBOHYDRATE
29g PROTEIN	21g FAT	0.7g FIBER

3 tbsp	(45 ml) butter
2	shallots, finely chopped
¼ tsp	(1 ml) tarragon
¼ lb	(125 g) mushrooms, finely chopped
1 tbsp	(15 ml) chopped parsley
3 tbsp	(45 ml) heavy cream
16	thin slices raw turkey breast, flattened
¼	red onion, in pieces
1	green pepper, in bite-size pieces
1 tbsp	(15 ml) lemon juice
	salt and pepper

1 The easiest way to flatten the turkey slices is with a mallet on waxed paper.

2 After shallots and tarragon have cooked for 2 minutes, add mushrooms and parsley; continue cooking 4 minutes over medium-high heat.

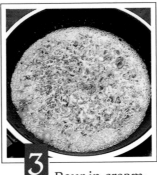

3 Pour in cream; mix and cook 2 to 3 minutes over high heat. Remove and cool slightly.

4 Spread about 1 tbsp (15 ml) of mushroom mixture over meat. Fold sides and roll.

Preheat oven to 400°F (200°C).

Heat 2 tbsp (30 ml) butter in frying pan. Cook shallots and tarragon 2 minutes.

Add mushrooms and parsley; continue cooking 4 minutes over medium-high heat. Season generously.

Pour in cream, mix and cook 2 to 3 minutes over high heat. Remove from heat and cool slightly.

Lay turkey slices flat on counter; spread about 1 tbsp (15 ml) of mushroom mixture over meat. Fold one side over and then the other side so that they overlap slightly. Start at one end and roll.

Alternate turkey rolls with onion and green pepper on skewers. Set aside in ovenproof platter.

Mix remaining butter with lemon juice; brush this over kebabs and season well.

Change oven setting to Grill (Broil) and cook 12 minutes 6 in (15 cm) from top element. Turn skewers over once and baste occasionally.

Strips of Beef and Vegetables

(serves 4)

1 SERVING	389 CALORIES	12g CARBOHYDRATE
47g PROTEIN	17g FAT	3.7g FIBER

2 tbsp	(30 ml) olive oil
1½ lb	(750 g) sirloin tip
3	garlic cloves, smashed and chopped
1	head broccoli (in flowerets), blanched 4 minutes
16	large cherry tomatoes
½	red onion, cut in 2 and sectioned
	juice 1 lemon
	salt and pepper

Heat 1 tsp (5 ml) oil in frying pan. When very hot, add whole piece of meat and sear on all sides. Season well.

Slice beef into ½ in (0.65 cm) strips. Place in bowl along with remaining oil, garlic and lemon juice. Marinate 15 minutes.

Drain beef and reserve marinade. Fold pieces in half and alternate on skewers along with vegetables.

Place on ovenproof platter and broil 6 minutes 6 in (15 cm) from top element. Turn skewers over once and baste several times with marinade.

Place remaining oil, garlic and lemon juice in bowl.

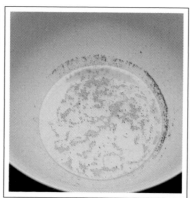

Drain beef and reserve marinade.

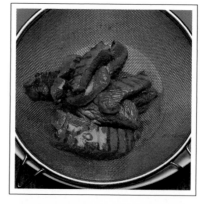

Add strips of beef and marinate 15 minutes.

Fold pieces of meat in half and alternate on skewers along with vegetables.

Meat and Potato Kebabs

(serves 4)

1 SERVING	441 CALORIES	27g CARBOHYDRATE
45g PROTEIN	17g FAT	4.8g FIBER

1 ½ lb	(750 g) sirloin steak, in 1 in (2.5 cm) long strips about ¾ in (2 cm) thick
3 tbsp	(45 ml) soya sauce
2	garlic cloves, smashed and chopped
2 tbsp	(30 ml) vegetable oil
16	small new round potatoes, peeled and cooked
2 tbsp	(30 ml) catsup
1 tbsp	(15 ml) honey
	salt and pepper

Preheat oven to 400°F (200°C).

Place beef, soya sauce, garlic and oil in bowl; marinate 15 minutes.

Alternate beef and potatoes on skewers; place on ovenproof platter.

Mix catsup with honey and brush over skewers; season generously. Broil 7 minutes in oven 6 in (15 cm) from top element. Turn skewers over once.

Serve with salad.

Beef Marinated in Bourbon

(serves 4)

1 SERVING	435 CALORIES	13g CARBOHYDRATE
53g PROTEIN	19g FAT	1.5g FIBER

2 lb	(900 g) sirloin tip, in 1 ¼ in (3 cm) cubes
¼ cup	(50 ml) bourbon
2 tbsp	(30 ml) soya sauce
1 tsp	(5 ml) Dijon mustard
¼ tsp	(1 ml) Worcestershire sauce
12	blanched mushroom caps
12	bite-size pieces bok choy (stem only)
2	white onions, cut in 4, blanched and sectioned
2	large carrots, cut in ½ in (1.2 cm) lengths and blanched
2 tbsp	(30 ml) vegetable oil
	salt and pepper

Marinate sirloin in mixture of bourbon, soya sauce, mustard and Worcestershire sauce for 1 hour.

Drain beef and reserve marinade. Alternate beef and vegetables on skewers and place on ovenproof platter; brush with oil.

Season skewers generously and broil 4 minutes in oven 4 in (10 cm) from top element. Turn skewers over once.

Move skewers 6 in (15 cm) from top element; finish broiling another 4 minutes turning skewers once. Baste with a bit of marinade.

Veal in Beer Marinade

(serves 4)

1 SERVING	186 CALORIES	11g CARBOHYDRATE
13g PROTEIN	10g FAT	1.4g FIBER

½ lb	(250 g) veal tenderloin, sliced in ¼ in (0.65 cm) thick round
1 cup	(250 ml) beer
1 tbsp	(15 ml) chopped fresh ginger
¼ tsp	(1 ml) Tabasco sauce
¼ tsp	(1 ml) Trinidad-style hot sauce
12	green onions, in 1 ¼ in (3 cm) long sticks
1	small zucchini, sliced ½ in (1.2 cm) thick
1	red pepper, in bite-size pieces
1 tbsp	(15 ml) vegetable oil
1 tbsp	(15 ml) honey
	salt and pepper

Marinate veal in mixture of beer, ginger, Tabasco, hot sauce and salt and pepper. Refrigerate 1 hour.

Drain veal and reserve marinade.

Alternate veal (fold each piece in two) along with onion sticks, zucchini and red pepper on skewers. Place in ovenproof dish and baste with marinade; sprinkle with oil and honey.

Broil 16 minutes in oven 6 in (15 cm) from top element. Turn skewers over twice.

Serve on rice.

1 Marinate veal in mixture of beer, ginger, Tabasco, hot sauce and salt and pepper. Refrigerate 1 hour.

2 Alternate veal pieces folded in two along with vegetables on skewers.

Veal Scallopini on Skewers

(serves 4)

1 SERVING	216 CALORIES	6g CARBOHYDRATE
12g PROTEIN	16g FAT	0g FIBER

4	veal scallopini from leg
3 tbsp	(45 ml) olive oil
2 tbsp	(30 ml) maple syrup
¼ tsp	(1 ml) tarragon
1 tbsp	(15 ml) wine vinegar
	few drops Trinidad-style hot sauce
	salt and pepper
	lemon juice to taste
	paprika to taste

If butcher has not already pounded veal, place pieces between two sheets of waxed paper. Flatten with mallet until very thin. Trim away fat and season generously.

Roll scallopini lengthwise keeping meat fairly taut. Secure each roll on very long skewer. Refer to Photo 2 for visual help.

Place skewers on ovenproof platter and set aside.

Mix oil, maple syrup, tarragon, vinegar, hot sauce, salt, pepper and lemon juice together.

Brush mixture over skewers and broil 7 minutes in oven 6 in (15 cm) from top element.

Turn skewers over and season with paprika; baste with maple syrup mixture. Continue broiling 7 minutes.

Remove veal from skewers.

Serve with green vegetables and garnish with broiled tomatoes.

If butcher has not already pounded veal, place pieces between two sheets of waxed paper. Flatten with mallet until very thin.

Depending on the length of your veal rolls the skewer need only be inserted twice in order to keep meat in place.

Veal and Mushroom Caps

(serves 4)

1 SERVING	285 CALORIES	4g CARBOHYDRATE
20g PROTEIN	21g FAT	0.6g FIBER

½ lb	(250 g) veal tenderloin, in bite-size pieces
12	mushroom caps, cleaned
12	bite-size chunks of celery
8	slices red onion
¼ cup	(50 ml) wine vinegar
2	garlic cloves, smashed and chopped
3 tbsp	(45 ml) olive oil
¼ tsp	(1 ml) fresh ground pepper
1 tsp	(5 ml) chopped parsley
9	bay leaves
3	½ in (1.2 cm) thick slices cooked back bacon, cubed and sautéed in butter

Place veal, mushrooms, celery and onion in bowl; set aside.

Place vinegar, garlic, oil, pepper, parsley and 1 bay leaf in small saucepan; bring to boil and cook 5 minutes over medium heat.

Pour hot liquid over veal and vegetables in bowl; marinate 1 hour on countertop. Drain and reserve marinade.

Alternate bacon, veal, mushrooms, celery, remaining bay leaves and onion on skewers. Place in ovenproof platter and broil 12 minutes 6 in (15 cm) from top element. Turn skewers over once and baste occasionally with marinade.

1 Place veal, mushrooms, celery and onion in bowl; set aside.

2 Pour hot marinade into bowl and leave on countertop for 1 hour.

Lemon Veal Kebabs

(serves 4)

1 SERVING	265 CALORIES	11g CARBOHYDRATE
17g PROTEIN	17g FAT	2.0g FIBER

½ lb	(250 g) veal tenderloin, sliced in ¼ in (0.65 cm) thick rounds
16	mushroom caps, cleaned
1	yellow pepper, in large pieces
¼ cup	(50 ml) olive oil
¼ cup	(50 ml) wine vinegar
1 tbsp	(15 ml) chopped fresh tarragon
2	broccoli stalks, cubed and cooked
½	red onion, in large pieces
	juice 1 lemon

Place veal, mushrooms and pepper in bowl. Sprinkle in oil, vinegar, tarragon and lemon juice. Refrigerate 35 minutes.

Drain and reserve marinade. Alternate veal (fold each piece in 2), mushrooms, yellow pepper, broccoli and onion on skewers.

Place in ovenproof dish and pour marinade over skewers. Broil 12 minutes in oven 6 in (15 cm) from top element. Turn skewers over once.

Serve with baked potatoes or other vegetables.

Marinate veal, mushrooms and pepper in a mixture of oil, vinegar, tarragon and lemon juice. Refrigerate for 35 minutes.

Alternate veal and vegetables on skewers. It is important to fold each piece of veal in two as you add them to the skewers.

Spicy Meatballs

Veal and Prune Kebabs

(serves 4)

1 SERVING	480 CALORIES	44g CARBOHYDRATE
40g PROTEIN	16g FAT	8.8g FIBER

1½ lb	(750 g) veal sirloin, cut in strips
½ cup	(125 ml) rice wine
2 tbsp	(30 ml) oil
1 tsp	(5 ml) lemon juice
24	pitted prunes
1½	green peppers, diced large
24	¾ in (2 cm) celery pieces, blanched
12	fresh mint leaves
	pinch thyme
	salt and fresh ground pepper

Place meat in wine, oil, lemon juice and thyme; marinate 15 minutes on countertop.

Drain meat and reserve marinade. Alternate veal, prunes, green peppers, celery and mint leaves on skewers; place on ovenproof platter.

Generously brush with marinade and broil 10 minutes 6 in (15 cm) from top element. Turn skewers over once and season during cooking.

(serves 4)

1 SERVING	490 CALORIES	21g CARBOHYDRATE
52g PROTEIN	22g FAT	0.5g FIBER

¾ lb	(375 g) lean ground pork
¾ lb	(375 g) lean ground veal
2 tbsp	(30 ml) chili sauce
3 tbsp	(45 ml) breadcrumbs
¼ tsp	(1 ml) chili powder
1	egg
1 tsp	(5 ml) Worcestershire sauce
¼ tsp	(1 ml) paprika
½ cup	(125 ml) chili sauce
½ cup	(125 ml) catsup
2 tbsp	(30 ml) oil
2 tbsp	(30 ml) sherry
	salt and pepper

Preheat oven to 400°F (200°C).

Place pork, veal, 2 tbsp (30 ml) chili sauce, breadcrumbs, chili powder, egg, Worcestershire sauce and paprika in mixer; process until meat forms a ball and sticks to sides of bowl.

Cover with waxed paper and chill 1 hour.

Dust hands with flour and shape mixture into small meatballs; thread on skewers. Place on ovenproof platter.

Mix remaining ingredients together. Cook skewers 8 minutes 6 in (15 cm) from top element; turn over once and baste often with sauce.

Dinner Party Skewers

(serves 4)

1 SERVING	215 CALORIES	21g CARBOHYDRATE
17g PROTEIN	7g FAT	1.1g FIBER

¼ cup	(50 ml) molasses
¼ cup	(50 ml) vinegar
1 tbsp	(15 ml) tomato paste
3	anchovy filets, chopped and mashed
1	large pork tenderloin, sliced thick
2	large celery stalks, in 1 in (2.5 cm) lengths
1	large green pepper, in bite-size pieces
1	seedless orange
	juice ½ lemon
	juice 1 orange

Preheat oven to 500°F (260°C).

Mix molasses, vinegar and tomato paste together in large bowl. Add lemon and orange juices, anchovies and mix very well.

Place pork, celery and green pepper in marinade; set aside 1 hour on countertop.

Slice other orange in two; cut each half into ¼ in (0.65 cm) thick slices. Do not peel.

Alternate double slices of orange along with ingredients in bowl on skewers; place on ovenproof platter.

Cook 14 minutes, turning skewers over once.

1 Mix molasses, vinegar and tomato paste together in large bowl. Add anchovies, lemon and orange juices; mix very well.

2 Place pork, celery and green pepper in marinade; set aside 1 hour on countertop.

Ribs and Tomatoes

(serves 4)

1 SERVING	383 CALORIES	16g CARBOHYDRATE
19g PROTEIN	27g FAT	0.9g FIBER

2½ lb	(1.2 kg) pork back ribs
3 tbsp	(45 ml) maple syrup
¼ cup	(50 ml) catsup
2	garlic cloves, smashed and chopped
1	large yellow pepper, in large pieces
6	slices precooked bacon, cut in half and rolled
1	tomato, in thin wedges
	juice ½ lemon
	few drops Tabasco sauce
	salt and pepper

Place ribs in large saucepan and cover with water; bring to boil. Skim and continue cooking 1 hour over medium heat.

Remove ribs from water and cool; cut into 1 in (2.5 cm) pieces.

Mix maple syrup, catsup, garlic, lemon juice, Tabasco, salt and pepper together in bowl. Stir in ribs and let stand 15 minutes on countertop.

Alternate rib pieces, yellow pepper, rolled bacon and tomato on skewers. Place in ovenproof platter and broil 8 minutes 6 in (15 cm) from top element. Turn skewers once and baste with leftover catsup mixture.

After ribs have been cooked in hot water, remove and cool. Then cut into 1 in (2.5 cm) pieces.

Alternate rib pieces, yellow pepper, rolled bacon and tomato on skewers.

Pork and Vegetable Kebabs

(serves 4)

1 SERVING	224 CALORIES	12g CARBOHYDRATE
17g PROTEIN	12g FAT	1.6g FIBER

5 oz	(142 g) piece Polish sausage
1	pork tenderloin, fat trimmed
1	small zucchini, in ½ in (1.2 cm) thick slices
1	yellow pepper, in bite-size pieces
8	green onions, in 1½ in (4 cm) long sticks
¼ tsp	(1 ml) Worcestershire sauce
½ cup	(125 ml) catsup
1 tsp	(5 ml) horseradish
	few drops Tabasco sauce
	salt and pepper

Preheat oven to 500°F (260°C).

Remove skin from sausage and slice in 1½ in (4 cm) rings. Cube pork tenderloin and place in bowl along with sausage, zucchini, yellow pepper and onion sticks.

Add Worcestershire sauce, catsup, horseradish, Tabasco sauce, salt and pepper to bowl; mix until everything is evenly coated. Marinate 15 minutes on countertop.

Alternate ingredients on skewers and place on ovenproof platter. Cook 15 minutes 6 in (15 cm) from top element turning skewers over twice.

Serve with potatoes if desired.

Prepare ingredients as directed in recipe then place them in a bowl.

2 Add Worcestershire sauce, catsup, horseradish, Tabasco sauce, salt and pepper to bowl; mix until everything is evenly coated. Marinate 15 minutes on countertop.

Pork Kebabs with Sweet-Sour Sauce

(serves 4)

1 SERVING	388 CALORIES	27g CARBOHYDRATE
34g PROTEIN	16g FAT	2.8g FIBER

1 tbsp	(15 ml) vegetable oil
1	garlic clove, smashed and chopped
1	small onion, thinly sliced
1	small carrot, thinly sliced
2	pineapple rings, cubed
2 tbsp	(30 ml) soya sauce
2 tbsp	(30 ml) wine vinegar
1 tbsp	(15 ml) sugar
3 tbsp	(45 ml) catsup
1 cup	(250 ml) hot chicken stock
1 tbsp	(15 ml) cornstarch
3 tbsp	(45 ml) cold water
1 lb	(500 g) pork tenderloin, in strips
16	baby carrots, blanched
1 ½	yellow peppers, diced large
	salt and pepper

To prepare sauce, heat oil in frying pan. When hot, cook garlic, onion and carrot 3 minutes over medium heat.

Stir in pineapple, soya sauce and vinegar; cook 2 minutes.

Add sugar and catsup; mix well. Pour in chicken stock, season and bring to boil.

Mix cornstarch with water; stir into sauce and cook 2 minutes. Remove from heat.

Fold pork strips in half and alternate along with baby carrots and pepper pieces on skewers. Season well and place on ovenproof platter.

Generously brush sweet-sour sauce over skewers; broil 4 to 5 minutes each side 6 in (15 cm) from top element. Baste frequently.

Ham and Apple on Skewers

(serves 4)

1 SERVING	355 CALORIES	37g CARBOHYDRATE
36g PROTEIN	7g FAT	2.5g FIBER

2	slices Virginia ham, ¾ in (2 cm) thick and in ¾ in (2 cm) cubes
3	apples, in wedges with skin
3 tbsp	(45 ml) maple syrup
2 tsp	(10 ml) soya sauce
½ cup	(125 ml) catsup
¼ cup	(50 ml) apple juice
	pinch cinnamon
	pinch ground clove

Place all ingredients in bowl, mix and marinate 15 minutes.

Drain and reserve marinade. Alternate ham and apples on skewers; place on ovenproof platter.

Broil 8 to 10 minutes 6 in (15 cm) from top element. Turn skewers over once and baste with marinade.

These kebabs are very tasty for brunch.

Cabbage Rolls on Skewers

(serves 4)

1 SERVING	334 CALORIES	5g CARBOHYDRATE
38g PROTEIN	18g FAT	0.6g FIBER

1 tbsp	(15 ml) butter
½ lb	(250 g) ground pork
½ lb	(250 g) ground veal
¼ tsp	(1 ml) paprika
¼ tsp	(1 ml) ground clove
½ cup	(125 ml) grated cheddar cheese
½ cup	(125 ml) cooked chopped onion
1 tbsp	(15 ml) chopped parsley
1 tbsp	(15 ml) sour cream
1	egg, lightly beaten
8	large cabbage leaves, blanched
	salt and pepper

Heat butter in frying pan. When hot, brown pork and veal 4 to 5 minutes over medium heat; season with paprika and clove.

Transfer meat to bowl and add remaining ingredients except cabbage leaves. Mix until well combined, cover and chill 1 hour.

Lay cabbage leaves flat and spread about 3 tbsp (45 ml) of meat mixture over each leaf. Roll fairly tight and tuck in ends. Place tube-like rolls on plate and weight down with another plate; chill 15 minutes.

Cut each cabbage roll into 3 pieces and carefully thread on skewers. Broil 6 to 8 minutes in oven 6 in (15 cm) from top element; turn skewers over once.

This unusual kebab dish also serves well topped with a hint of tomato sauce.

Italian Sausage and Beef Kebabs

(serves 4)

1 SERVING	611 CALORIES	17g CARBOHYDRATE
39g PROTEIN	43g FAT	1.3g FIBER

1 lb	(500 g) sirloin tip, in bite-size pieces
1 lb	(500 g) Italian sausage, in ¾ in (2 cm) pieces
2	onions, cut in 4 and sectioned
1½	red peppers, in bite-size pieces
8	garlic cloves, peeled
½ cup	(125 ml) olive oil
¼ cup	(50 ml) chili sauce
	juice 1 lemon
	fresh ground pepper
	dash paprika

Alternate beef, sausage, onion, pepper and garlic on skewers. Place on ovenproof platter.

Mix oil, chili sauce, lemon juice, pepper and paprika together; brush over skewers.

Broil about 6 minutes on each side (depending on size) 6 in (15 cm) from top element. Baste once or twice.

Accompany with a spicy rice.

Polish Sausages and Bacon

(serves 4)

1 SERVING	169 CALORIES	10g CARBOHYDRATE
12g PROTEIN	9g FAT	0.8g FIBER

2	¾ in (2 cm) thick slices back bacon, diced large
½	red onion, cut in 3
4 oz	(115 g) Polish sausage, peeled and diced large
½	cucumber, peeled, seeded and cut in ¾ in (2 cm) thick slices
½ cup	(125 ml) catsup
1 tbsp	(15 ml) horseradish
	juice 1 lime
	few drops Tabasco sauce
	pepper

Preheat oven to 500°F (260°C).

Alternate bacon, onion, sausage and cucumber on skewers; place on ovenproof platter.

Mix remaining ingredients together and brush over skewers.

Cook 14 minutes 8 in (20 cm) from top element. Turn skewers over once and baste with leftover catsup mixture if desired.

Cocktail Sausages on Skewers

(serves 4)

1 SERVING	320 CALORIES	7g CARBOHYDRATE
10g PROTEIN	28g FAT	0.5g FIBER

8	slices bacon, precooked 2 minutes
8 oz	(230 g) can cocktail sausages
10 oz	(284 ml) can mandarin sections, drained
	barbecue sauce for basting

Cut bacon slices in two and roll; alternate along with sausages and mandarins on thin wooden skewers.

Place in ovenproof dish and baste with barbecue sauce. Broil 5 minutes in oven 6 in (15 cm) from top element.

Serve as an appetizer or snack.

Tasty Lamb Kebabs

(serves 4)

1 SERVING	266 CALORIES	10g CARBOHYDRATE
16g PROTEIN	18g FAT	0.4g FIBER

½ cup	(125 ml) mint sauce
1 tbsp	(15 ml) olive oil
2	garlic cloves, smashed and chopped
8	small lamb chops, ½ in (1.2 cm) thick, boned and fat removed
2	small onions, cut in 4 and sectioned
10	bay leaves
1½	celery stalks, cut in 1 in (2.5 cm) lengths and blanched
	salt and pepper
	juice ¼ lemon

Preheat oven to 400°F (200°C).

Place mint sauce, oil, garlic, pepper and lemon juice in bowl. Add lamb and mix thoroughly; marinate 15 minutes on countertop.

Alternate lamb, onion sections, bay leaves and celery pieces on skewers; season generously. Place on ovenproof platter.

Change oven setting to broil. Cook skewers 3 minutes each side 6 in (15 cm) from top element. Leave door ajar and baste with leftover mint marinade.

Serve with hot mustard if desired.

Hearty Lamb Kebabs

(serves 4)

1 SERVING	733 CALORIES	20g CARBOHYDRATE
44g PROTEIN	53g FAT	2.9g FIBER

2 lb	(900 g) boneless leg of lamb, in ¾ in (2 cm) pieces
2	onions, finely chopped
1 tbsp	(15 ml) crushed rosemary
½ cup	(125 ml) olive oil
2	bay leaves
1	large Spanish onion, cut in 8 and sectioned
1 tbsp	(15 ml) olive oil
2	garlic cloves, smashed and chopped
3	tomatoes, peeled and chopped
4	slices Italian bread, toasted
¼ cup	(50 ml) grated Parmesan cheese
	salt and pepper

Place lamb, chopped onions, rosemary, ¼ cup (125 ml) oil and bay leaves in bowl; mix and marinate 1 hour on countertop.

Alternate pieces of lamb and Spanish onion on skewers; place on ovenproof platter and set aside.

Heat remaining measure of oil in frying pan. Cook garlic and tomatoes 7 to 9 minutes over medium heat; season well. Reduce heat and simmer.

Place skewers in oven and broil 5 to 6 minutes 6 in (15 cm) from top element.

Spread tomato mixture over toasted bread slices and top with cheese; place in ovenproof dish.

Turn skewers over; broil another 5 to 6 minutes. Place bread beside skewers and broil, but for only 3 to 4 minutes.

To serve place one skewer on each slice of bread.

Salmon and Cucumber Kebabs

(serves 4)

1 SERVING	171 CALORIES	1g CARBOHYDRATE
26g PROTEIN	7g FAT	0.6g FIBER

2 tbsp	(30 ml) grated lemon rind
½ cup	(125 ml) dry white wine
1 tsp	(5 ml) tarragon
3	salmon steaks
½	English cucumber, peeled and diced large
8	fresh mint leaves
	juice 1 lemon
	salt and pepper

Mix lemon rind, wine, tarragon and lemon juice together in large bowl.

Remove middle bone from salmon steaks, leave on skin and cut in 2. Cut each half into 3 pieces. Add to bowl along with cucumber; marinate 15 minutes.

Drain and reserve marinade.

Alternate salmon, cucumber and mint leaves on skewers; place on ovenproof platter and season.

Broil 4 minutes 6 in (15 cm) from top element; baste once with marinade.

Turn skewers over and broil about 3 minutes, depending on size. Baste once more.

Perch Kebabs

(serves 4)

1 SERVING	392 CALORIES	8g CARBOHYDRATE
45g PROTEIN	20g FAT	1.1g FIBER

2	garlic cloves, smashed and chopped
1 tbsp	(15 ml) oyster sauce
2 lb	(900 g) perch filets, cut in half then in 1 in (2.5 cm) pieces
8	cherry tomatoes
4	small onions, blanched and cut in 4
3 tbsp	(45 ml) olive oil
2 tbsp	(30 ml) sherry
	juice 1 lemon
	salt and pepper

Preheat oven to 400°F (200°C).

Mix garlic, oyster sauce and lemon juice in bowl. Add fish and marinate 15 minutes.

Roll fish pieces and alternate along with tomatoes and onions on skewers. Place on ovenproof platter.

Mix oil and sherry together; brush over skewers. Season to taste.

Change oven setting to broil. Cook skewers 3 minutes each side 6 in (15 cm) from top element.

1 Mix garlic, oyster sauce and lemon in bowl.

2 Add fish and marinate 15 minutes.

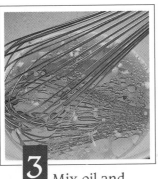

3 Mix oil and sherry together.

4 Brush sherry mixture over skewers before broiling.

Sturgeon, Brussels Sprouts and Carrots

(serves 4)

1 SERVING	254 CALORIES	18g CARBOHYDRATE
23g PROTEIN	10g FAT	4.8g FIBER

2	sturgeon steaks, ¾ in (2 cm) thick and in ¾ in (2 cm) cubes
24	cooked Brussels sprouts
24	cooked baby carrots
½ cup	(125 ml) sake
2 tbsp	(30 ml) oil
1	garlic clove, smashed and chopped
8	oyster mushrooms
	salt and pepper

Place fish, sprouts, carrots, sake, oil, garlic, salt and pepper in bowl; marinate 15 minutes.

Drain and reserve marinade. Alternate fish and vegetables on skewers. Note: It is best to fold mushrooms in half.

Place skewers on ovenproof platter and broil 8 to 10 minutes 6 in (15 cm) from top element. Turn skewers over once and baste with marinade.

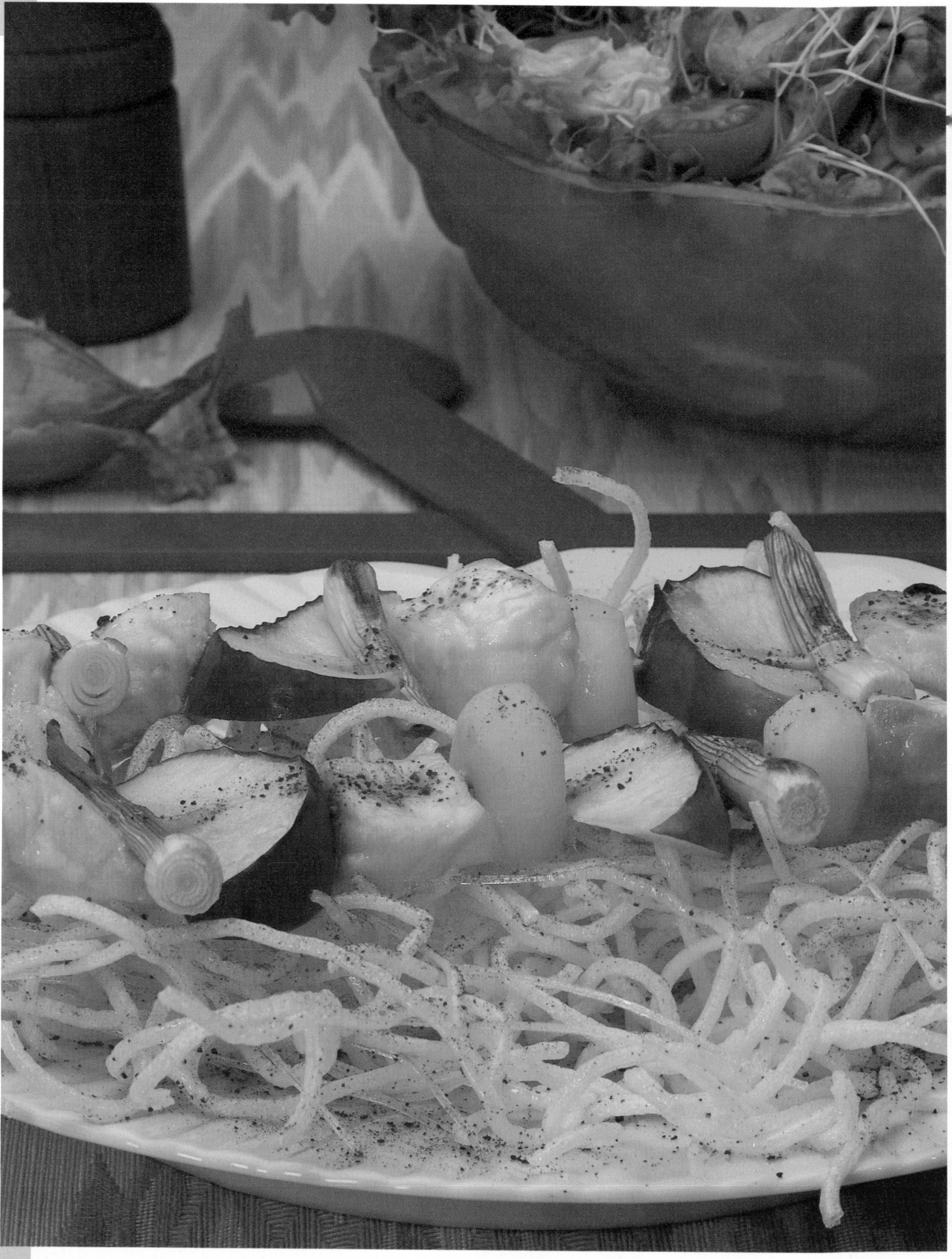

Clam Kebabs

Fish Lover's Kebabs

(serves 4)

1 SERVING	385 CALORIES	10g CARBOHYDRATE
48g PROTEIN	17g FAT	1.0g FIBER

2 lb	(900 g) halibut steaks, ¾ in (2 cm) thick and in 1 in (2.5 cm) pieces
1	onion, finely chopped
4 tbsp	(60 ml) oil
2 tbsp	(30 ml) lime juice
¼ tsp	(1 ml) Tabasco sauce
¼ cup	(50 ml) dry white wine
6	green onions, in 1 in (2.5 cm) sticks
7 oz	(199 ml) can water chestnuts, drained
12	lime slices
12	apple wedges with skin

Marinate halibut 15 minutes in chopped onion, oil, lime juice, Tabasco sauce and wine.

Drain and reserve marinade.

Alternate fish, green onions, water chestnuts, lime slices and apple wedges on skewers. Place on ovenproof platter.

Broil 8 to 10 minutes in oven 6 in (15 cm) from top element. Turn skewers over once and baste occasionally with marinade.

(serves 4)

1 SERVING	406 CALORIES	33g CARBOHYDRATE
28g PROTEIN	18g FAT	0.2g FIBER

24	large clams, scrubbed
1 tsp	(5 ml) lemon juice
1 tbsp	(15 ml) teriyaki sauce
1 cup	(250 ml) seasoned flour
2	beaten eggs
1 ½ cups	(375 ml) crushed Corn Flakes
	melted garlic butter
	pepper

Preheat oven to 450°F (240°C).

Spread clams in one layer in large roasting pan. Place in oven for 4 to 5 minutes or until shells open.

Shuck and discard shells. Place clams in bowl with lemon juice and teriyaki sauce; mix well and season with pepper.

Dredge clams in flour, dip in eggs and coat with corn flakes. Put on skewers with skewer going through each clam twice. Set all on ovenproof platter.

Change oven setting to broil. Baste skewers with garlic butter, leave oven door ajar, and broil 6 minutes 6 in (15 cm) from top element. Turn skewers over once and baste again if necessary.

Oyster Kebabs

(serves 4)

1 SERVING	681 CALORIES	50g CARBOHYDRATE
55g PROTEIN	29g FAT	0g FIBER

36	large shucked oysters
8	slices cooked bacon, cut in half
1 cup	(250 ml) flour
¼ tsp	(1 ml) paprika
1 tsp	(5 ml) chopped parsley
4 tbsp	(60 ml) butter, melted
¼ tsp	(1 ml) teriyaki sauce
	salt
	juice 1 lemon

Preheat oven to 400°F (200°C).

Alternate oysters and rolled pieces of bacon on skewers.

Mix flour with paprika and parsley. Roll skewers in this and place in ovenproof platter.

Mix butter, teriyaki sauce, salt and lemon juice together; pour over skewers. Change oven setting to broil and cook skewers 3 minutes each side 6 in (15 cm) from top element.

Serve with garlic bread.

Brandy Jumbo Shrimp

(serves 4)

1 SERVING	164 CALORIES	6g CARBOHYDRATE
17g PROTEIN	8g FAT	0.8g FIBER

20	raw jumbo shrimp, shelled and deveined
2	garlic cloves, smashed and chopped
½ cup	(125 ml) brandy
2 tbsp	(30 ml) olive oil
4	stems bok choy, in ¾ in (2 cm) pieces
	juice 1 lemon
	salt and pepper

Place all ingredients in bowl and marinate 30 minutes on countertop.

Alternate shrimp and bok choy on skewers. Place on ovenproof platter.

Broil 12 to 14 minutes in oven 6 in (15 cm) from top element. Turn skewers over once and season during cooking. Baste with marinade if desired.

Serve with tartare sauce.

Breaded Mussels on Skewers

(serves 4)

1 SERVING	610 CALORIES	60g CARBOHYDRATE
43g PROTEIN	22g FAT	0.2g FIBER

6½ lb	(3 kg) mussels, scrubbed and bearded
½ cup	(125 ml) dry white wine
4 tbsp	(60 ml) butter
1 tbsp	(15 ml) lemon juice
1 cup	(250 ml) seasoned flour
2	beaten eggs
2 cups	(500 ml) breadcrumbs
	few drops Tabasco sauce
	few drops lemon juice
	salt and pepper

Place mussels, wine, 2 tbsp (30 ml) butter, lemon juice and pepper in saucepan. Cover and bring to boil; continue cooking over medium heat until shells open.

Drain liquid into small bowl. Shuck mussels and pour any juices from shells into the small bowl. Set aside.

Dredge mussels in flour. Dip several at a time in eggs then coat with breadcrumbs.

Thread on wooden skewers and place on ovenproof platter. Broil 4 minutes very close to top element; turn skewers once.

Meanwhile, prepare sauce by transferring reserved mussel liquid in bowl to saucepan. Reduce by ⅔ over medium-high heat.

Stir in remaining butter, Tabasco sauce and few drops lemon juice; cook 1 minute.

Serve with kebabs.

Chinese Shrimp Kebabs

(serves 4)

1 SERVING	237 CALORIES	21g CARBOHYDRATE
27g PROTEIN	5g FAT	0g FIBER

16	chunks fresh pineapple
2 lb	(900 g) raw shrimp, shelled and deveined
24	fresh snow peas, blanched
½ cup	(125 ml) rice wine
2 tbsp	(30 ml) sesame sauce
1 tbsp	(15 ml) oil
1 tsp	(5 ml) lime juice
	salt and pepper

Preheat oven to 400°F (200°C).

Place pineapple, shrimp, pea pods, wine and sesame sauce in bowl; marinate 15 minutes.

Alternate ingredients on skewers and place on ovenproof platter. Mix oil with lime juice; set aside.

Cook skewers 6 to 8 minutes in oven 6 in (15 cm) from top element. Baste occasionally with oil mixture and turn skewers over once. Season to taste.

Serve with steamed rice and chopsticks.

Escargot Appetizer

(serves 4)

1 SERVING	462 CALORIES	20g CARBOHYDRATE
19g PROTEIN	34g FAT	0.2g FIBER

24	canned snails, drained
8	slices bacon, precooked and in 2 in (5 cm) pieces
16	cooked pearl onions
½ cup	(125 ml) melted garlic butter
1 ½ cups	(375 ml) seasoned breadcrumbs

Alternate snails, rolled pieces of bacon and pearl onions on short skewers. Place on ovenproof platter and baste generously with garlic butter.

Roll skewers in breadcrumbs until well coated. Broil 4 to 6 minutes in oven 4 in (10 cm) from top element. Turn skewers over once.

Serve with extra garlic butter and lemon wedges.

Scallop Kebabs with Fried Parsley

(serves 4)

1 SERVING	434 CALORIES	10g CARBOHYDRATE
31g PROTEIN	30g FAT	0.8g FIBER

½ cup	(125 ml) olive oil
3 tbsp	(45 ml) wine vinegar
½ tsp	(2 ml) crushed rosemary
2 tbsp	(30 ml) lemon juice
1 ½ lb	(750 g) large scallops
12	bay leaves
1	large lemon, sliced (remove seeds)
1	bunch fresh parsley
	fresh ground pepper

Reserve 3 tbsp (45 ml) oil. Place remaining oil in bowl along with vinegar, rosemary, lemon juice, scallops and pepper. Toss and marinate 1 hour on countertop.

Drain scallops and set marinade aside.

Alternate scallops, bay leaves and lemon slices on skewers; place on ovenproof platter.

Broil 3 minutes each side in oven 6 in (15 cm) from top element. Baste occasionally with marinade.

Before kebabs are done, heat reserved oil in frying pan. When hot, sauté parsley (as is, in bunch) about 2 minutes.

Serve as an unusual garnish with kebabs.

Stuffed Mushroom Caps

(serves 4)

1 SERVING	552 CALORIES	43g CARBOHYDRATE
32g PROTEIN	28g FAT	1.3g FIBER

1 lb	(500 g) ricotta cheese
¼ lb	(125 g) grated mozzarella cheese
1 tbsp	(15 ml) chopped parsley
¼ tsp	(1 ml) basil
32	blanched mushroom caps
2	beaten eggs
2 cups	(500 ml) seasoned breadcrumbs
	dash paprika
	salt and pepper
	Tabasco sauce to taste

Mix both cheeses, parsley, basil, paprika, salt, pepper and Tabasco together. Stuff mushroom caps.

Press two mushroom caps together (to keep stuffing in place) and thread 4 sets on each skewer.

Roll skewers in beaten eggs, then in breadcrumbs. Place on ovenproof platter and broil 6 minutes in oven 6 in (15 cm) from top element. Turn skewers over once.

Serve as an appetizer or with a main dish.

Mushroom Garnish

(serves 4)

1 SERVING	208 CALORIES	10g CARBOHYDRATE
24g PROTEIN	8g FAT	1.0g FIBER

1 tbsp	(15 ml) butter
1	onion, finely chopped
½ lb	(250 g) lean ground beef
1 tbsp	(15 ml) chopped parsley
¼ cup	(50 ml) grated Gruyère cheese
16	large mushrooms caps, blanched 3 minutes
3 tbsp	(45 ml) seasoned breadcrumbs
	salt and pepper

Heat butter in frying pan. Sauté onion 2 to 3 minutes over medium-low heat.

Add beef and parsley; season to taste. Continue cooking 3 to 4 minutes.

Mix in cheese and cook 1 minute. Remove from heat and stuff mushroom caps.

Thread mushroom caps on skewers with stuffing side up. Place on ovenproof platter and sprinkle breadcrumbs over stuffing.

Broil 3 to 4 minutes in oven 6 in (15 cm) from top element. Do not turn skewers over!

Serve as a vegetable garnish.

Assorted Pepper Kebabs

(serves 4)

1 SERVING	155 CALORIES	12g CARBOHYDRATE
2g PROTEIN	11g FAT	2.1g FIBER

4 tbsp	(60 ml) olive oil
¼ tsp	(1 ml) Tabasco sauce
½ tsp	(2 ml) lemon juice
2	garlic cloves, smashed and finely chopped
2	green peppers, seeded and halved
2	yellow peppers, seeded and halved
2	red peppers, seeded and halved
	freshly ground pepper

Preheat oven to 450°F (240°C).

Mix oil, Tabasco, lemon juice, garlic and pepper together. Place peppers in ovenproof dish and pour in mixture. Cook 10 minutes in middle of oven.

Remove and let cool slightly.

Cut pepper halves into 3 and alternate colours on skewers; brush with oil mixture. Broil 6 minutes 6 in (15 cm) from top element; turn over once.

Serve.

Eggplant and Bacon Skewers

(serves 4)

1 SERVING	88 CALORIES	9g CARBOHYDRATE
4g PROTEIN	4g FAT	0.8g FIBER

2	eggplant slices, ¾ in (2 cm) thick
1	back bacon slice, ¾ in (2 cm) thick
8	pieces of red onion
8	cherry tomatoes
¼ tsp	(1 ml) Worcestershire sauce
1 tbsp	(15 ml) oil
3 tbsp	(45 ml) plum sauce
	salt and pepper

Cut eggplant and bacon into ½ in (1.2 cm) cubes. Alternate along with onion and tomatoes on thin wooden skewers.

Place in ovenproof dish and season generously. Sprinkle on Worcestershire sauce, oil and plum sauce.

Broil 10 minutes in oven 6 in (15 cm) from top element. Turn skewers over once.

Cut eggplant and bacon into ½ in (1.2 cm) cubes.

Alternate along with onion and tomatoes on thin wooden skewers. Place in ovenproof dish and season generously. Sprinkle in Worcestershire sauce, oil and plum sauce.

New Potatoes

(serves 4)

1 SERVING	548 CALORIES	34g CARBOHYDRATE
22g PROTEIN	36g FAT	7.1g FIBER

24	new round potatoes, cooked in jackets
24	slices bacon, medium cooked
1 cup	(250 ml) finely grated cheddar cheese
	dash paprika
	fresh ground pepper

Wrap potatoes with bacon slices and place on skewers. Set on ovenproof platter.

Broil 3 minutes in oven 6 in (15 cm) from top element. Turn skewers over; sprinkle with cheese, paprika and pepper. Finish broiling another 3 minutes.

Serve with meat or fish.

Mixed Vegetable Kebabs

(serves 4)

1 SERVING	74 CALORIES	12g CARBOHYDRATE
2g PROTEIN	2g FAT	2.1g FIBER

2	red peppers, in bite-size pieces
1	zucchini, cut in two and sliced thick
1	red onion, in large pieces
2 tbsp	(30 ml) soya sauce
1 tsp	(5 ml) Worcestershire sauce
1 tsp	(5 ml) oil
2	garlic cloves, smashed and chopped
½ tsp	(2 ml) tarragon
½ cup	(125 ml) barbecue sauce

Preheat oven to 450°F (240°C).

Place vegetables in bowl. Add soya sauce, Worcestershire sauce, oil, garlic and tarragon. Marinate 30 minutes at room temperature.

Drain vegetables and reserve marinade.

Alternate vegetables on skewers and place on ovenproof platter; baste with barbecue sauce.

Cook 8 minutes in oven 4 in (10 cm) from top element. Baste several times with marinade and turn skewers twice.

Serve with barbecue sauce for dipping.

1 Place red peppers, zucchini and onion in bowl.

2 Add soya sauce, Worcestershire sauce, oil, garlic and tarragon; marinate 30 minutes at room temperature.

Tomato Fruit Kebabs

(serves 4)

1 SERVING	140 CALORIES	34g CARBOHYDRATE
1g PROTEIN	0g FAT	2.7g FIBER

2	small bananas, sliced thick
¼	pineapple, in large chunks
1	apple, peeled and sliced in wedges
1	large tomato, cored and sliced in wedges
1 tbsp	(15 ml) brown sugar
1 tsp	(5 ml) cinnamon
2 tbsp	(30 ml) maple syrup

Place fruit, tomato, brown sugar, cinnamon and maple syrup in bowl; toss gently. Set aside 15 minutes on countertop.

Alternate pineapple, tomato, banana and apple on thin wooden skewers; repeat until ingredients are used.

Place on ovenproof platter and pour juices from bowl over kebabs. Broil 6 minutes in oven 6 in (15 cm) from top element. Turn skewers over once.

Serve as an interesting dessert or with a meat dish.

Pineapple Chunks and Water Chestnuts

(serves 4)

1 SERVING	143 CALORIES	15g CARBOHYDRATE
5g PROTEIN	7g FAT	0.4g FIBER

16	chunks fresh pineapple
8	slices bacon, medium cooked and cut in half
12	canned water chestnuts
2 tbsp	(30 ml) maple syrup
1 tsp	(5 ml) lemon juice

Wrap pineapple chunks with bacon. Alternate with water chestnuts on skewers and place on ovenproof platter.

Mix maple syrup with lemon juice; brush over skewers. Broil 3 minutes each side in oven 6 in (15 cm) from top element.

Serve as an appetizer or as a snack.

Apricot Dessert

(serves 4)

1 SERVING	259 CALORIES	47g CARBOHYDRATE
2g PROTEIN	7g FAT	2.9g FIBER

24	apricots, pitted
½ cup	(125 ml) Tia Maria
2 tbsp	(30 ml) butter
2 tbsp	(30 ml) sugar
	juice 1 orange
	juice ½ lemon
	whipped cream for topping

Marinate apricots in Tia Maria for 30 minutes.

Drain and reserve liquid; thread apricots on skewers.

Heat butter in frying pan. Stir in sugar and cook until golden brown; stir constantly!

Pour in reserved marinade and flambé. Add orange and lemon juices; cook 2 minutes.

Pour sauce into fairly deep baking dish and place skewers on top. Broil 6 minutes in oven.

Top with whipped cream if desired.

Double Orange Skewer Dessert

(serves 4)

1 SERVING	400 CALORIES	70g CARBOHYDRATE
3g PROTEIN	12g FAT	2.4g FIBER

2	mandarins, peeled and sectioned
1	seedless orange, peeled and sectioned
½	orange honeydew melon, cut in bite-size pieces
2 tbsp	(30 ml) granulated sugar
2 tbsp	(30 ml) orange liqueur
2 oz	(60 g) unsweetened chocolate
¼ cup	(50 ml) heavy cream
1 cup	(250 ml) icing sugar
	few drops vanilla

Place fruit in bowl with granulated sugar and liqueur. Toss and let stand while you make the sauce.

Place chocolate, cream, icing sugar and vanilla in double boiler. Cook until mixture is completely melted; stir constantly.

Alternate fruit on wooden skewers and place on individual dessert plates. Drizzle chocolate sauce over kebabs and serve.

Passion Fruit Kebabs

(serves 4)

1 SERVING	141 CALORIES	29g CARBOHYDRATE
4g PROTEIN	1g FAT	0g FIBER

4	passion fruit*, cut in half
2 tbsp	(30 ml) orange liqueur
2	egg whites
2 tbsp	(30 ml) sugar

Carefully thread fruit halves on short skewers. Sprinkle liqueur over each and place on ovenproof platter.

Beat egg whites until fairly stiff. Slowly incorporate sugar and continue beating 1½ minutes.

Spoon a large dollop of egg whites on each fruit half. Broil 2 minutes in oven 6 in (15 cm) from top element.

Serve immediately. Diners should eat passion fruit with a spoon.

* Choose your passion fruit carefully. Look for dark purple skin with a lumpy texture that is fairly firm.

Strawberry and Kiwi Kebabs

(serves 4)

1 SERVING	104 CALORIES	23g CARBOHYDRATE
3g PROTEIN	0g FAT	1.2g FIBER

24	ripe strawberries, hulled
4	ripe kiwis, peeled and cut in 4
3 tbsp	(45 ml) sugar
¼ cup	(50 ml) Lamb's Caribbean Cream
1 tbsp	(15 ml) grated lemon rind
2	egg whites

Preheat oven to 400°F (200°C).

Place strawberries and kiwis in bowl; add 1 tbsp (15 ml) sugar, Caribbean Cream and lemon rind. Toss and marinate 1 hour.

Alternate fruit on wooden skewers and place on ovenproof platter.

Beat egg whites until fairly stiff. Slowly incorporate remaining sugar and continue beating 1½ minutes.

Carefully arrange dollops of egg whites on top portion of skewers. Change oven setting to broil and brown 2 to 3 minutes 6 in (15 cm) from top element.

Serve immediately.

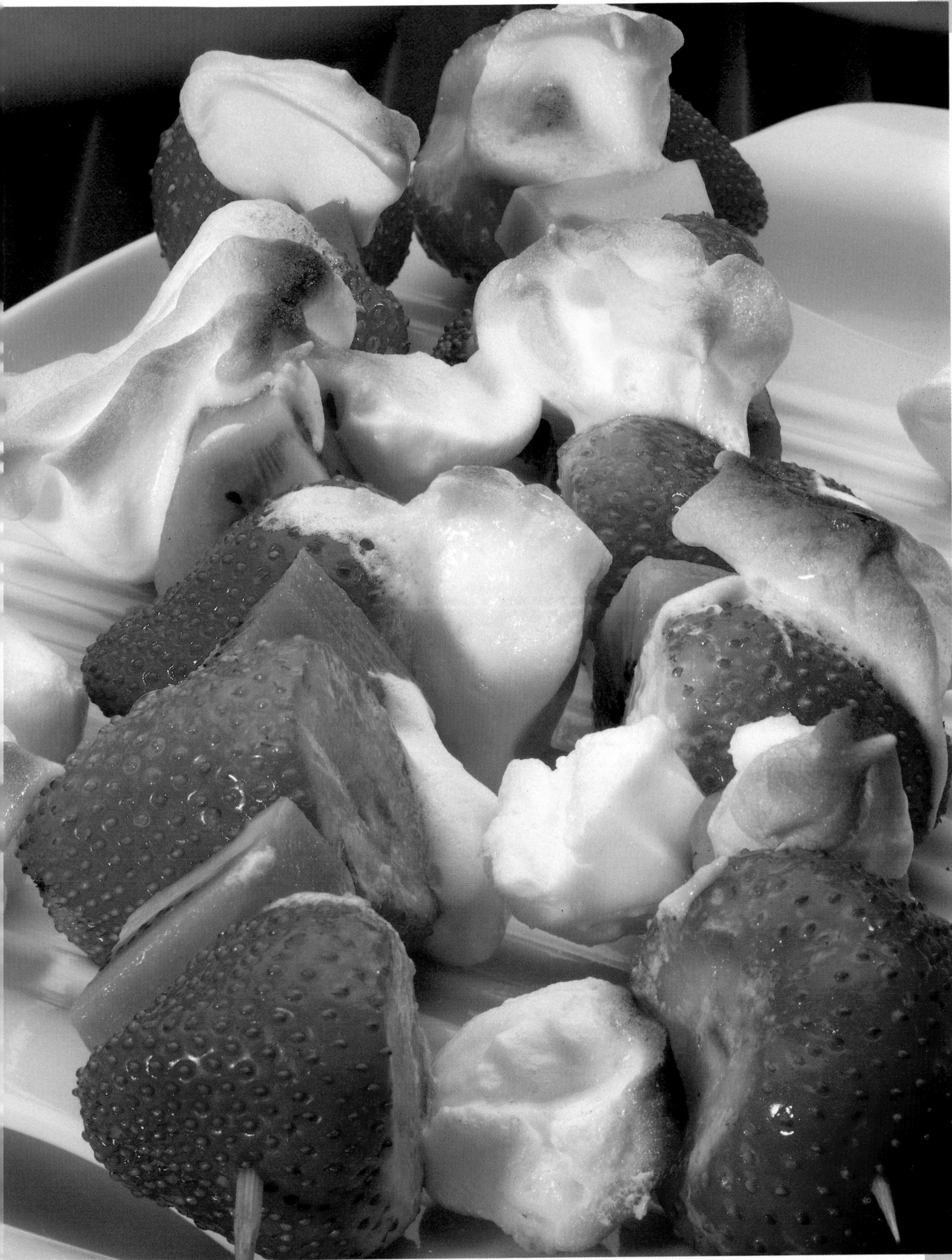

Skewer Sundae

(serves 4)

1 SERVING	429 CALORIES	54g CARBOHYDRATE
6g PROTEIN	21g FAT	1.6g FIBER

1	banana, sliced
12	strawberries, cut in half
12	chunks fresh pineapple
8	scoops French vanilla ice cream
2 tbsp	(30 ml) butter
2 tbsp	(30 ml) sugar
½ cup	(125 ml) orange juice
	grated rind ½ lemon
	grated rind ½ orange

Alternate fruit on short wooden skewers. Divide ice cream scoops between four sundae dishes and set skewers on top; refrigerate.

Heat butter in frying pan. Stir in sugar and cook until golden brown; mix constantly!

Add orange juice and rinds; continue cooking to reduce by half.

Cool slightly then pour over kebabs and serve.

Plums with Jubilee Sauce

(serves 4)

1 SERVING	175 CALORIES	36g CARBOHYDRATE
1g PROTEIN	3g FAT	2.9g FIBER

8	ripe plums, pitted and cut in half
¼ cup	(50 ml) kirsch
1 tbsp	(15 ml) butter
2 tbsp	(30 ml) sugar
¾ cup	(175 ml) cherry juice
½ cup	(125 ml) canned cherries
1 tsp	(5 ml) cornstarch
2 tbsp	(30 ml) cold water
	juice 1 orange

Marinate plums in half of kirsch for 10 minutes. Drain and reserve marinade; thread plum halves on short wooden skewers.

Heat butter with sugar in frying pan. Stir constantly and cook 1 minute.

Add cherry juice, cherries and orange juice; mix well. Add remaining kirsch and marinade; bring to boil.

Set skewers in sauce and cook 2 to 3 minutes over medium heat. Transfer skewers to dessert dishes and continue cooking sauce 2 to 3 minutes.

Mix cornstarch with water; stir into sauce and cook 1 minute.

Pour over kebabs and serve.

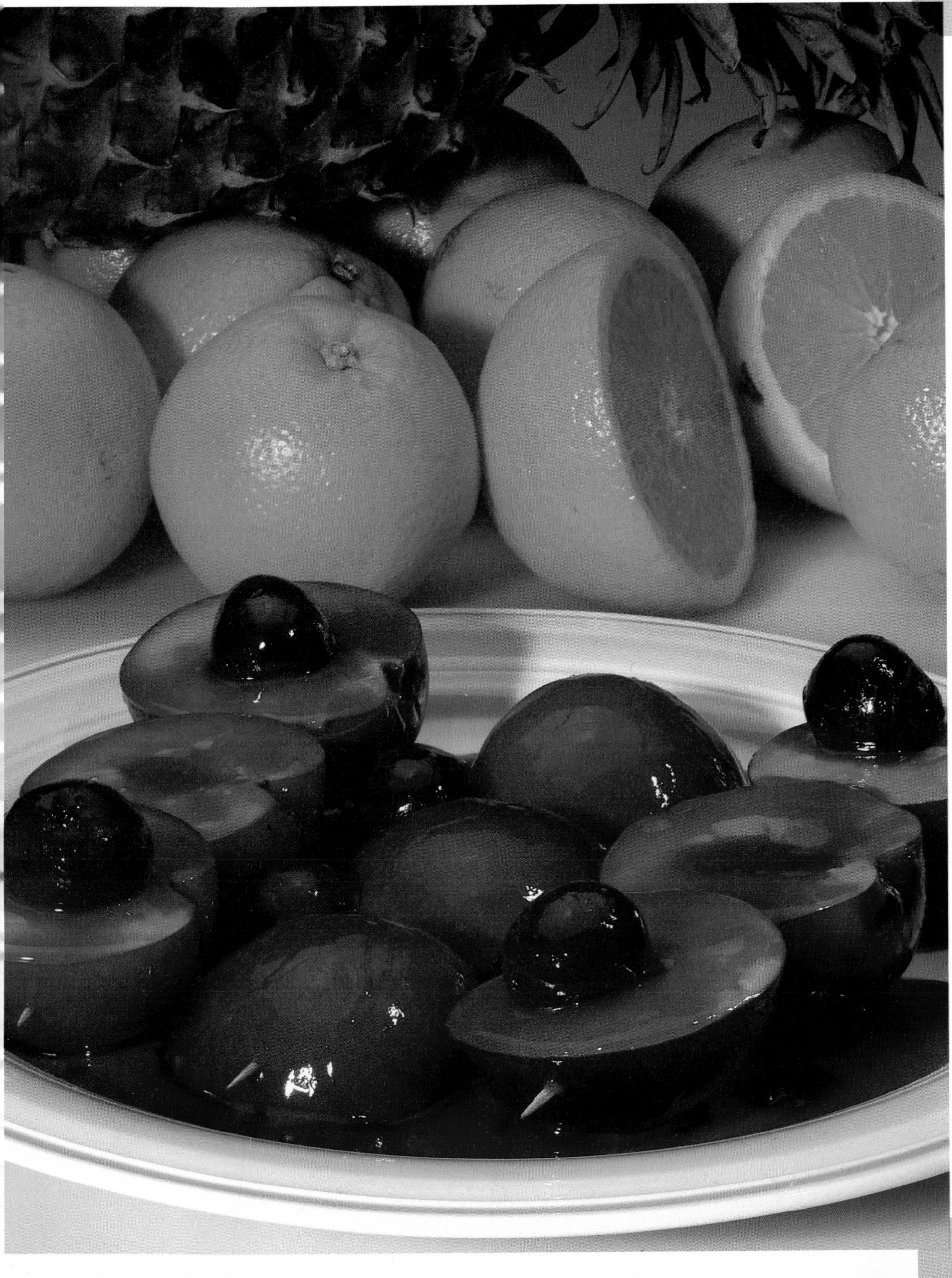

Onion Mustard Sauce

1 SERVING	17 CALORIES	2g CARBOHYDRATE
0g PROTEIN	1g FAT	0.1g FIBER

1 tbsp	(15 ml) olive oil
1	onion, chopped
¼ cup	(50 ml) wine vinegar
2 tbsp	(30 ml) capers
1 tsp	(5 ml) chopped parsley
¼ tsp	(1 ml) fresh ground pepper
1 cup	(250 ml) dry red wine
1½ cups	(375 ml) brown sauce, heated
2 tbsp	(30 ml) Dijon mustard

Heat oil in deep frying pan. When hot, add onion and cook 3 minutes over medium heat.

Stir in vinegar, capers, parsley and pepper; cook 3 minutes.

Pour in wine and cook 6 to 7 minutes over high heat.

Mix in brown sauce, correct seasoning and simmer 6 to 7 minutes over low heat.

Remove pan from stove, stir in mustard and serve sauce with beef or veal.

After onion has **1** cooked 3 minutes, stir in vinegar, capers, parsley and pepper; continue cooking 3 minutes.

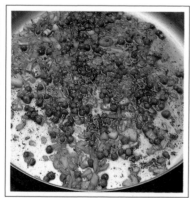

3 Mix in brown sauce, correct seasoning and simmer 6 to 7 minutes over low heat.

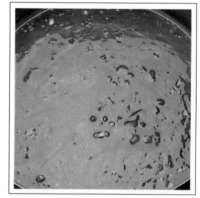

Pour in wine and **2** cook 6 to 7 minutes over high heat.

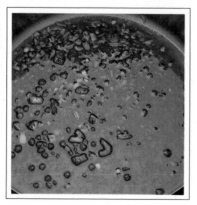

4 Remove pan from stove and stir in mustard before serving.

Parsley Sauce

1 SERVING	13 CALORIES	1g CARBOHYDRATE
0g PROTEIN	1g FAT	0g FIBER

1 tbsp	(15 ml) butter
2 tbsp	(30 ml) chopped parsley
1 tsp	(5 ml) oregano
1 tbsp	(15 ml) tarragon
2	shallots, chopped
2 tbsp	(30 ml) wine vinegar
½ cup	(125 ml) dry white wine
1 ½ cups	(375 ml) hot chicken stock
1 tbsp	(15 ml) cornstarch
3 tbsp	(45 ml) cold water
	salt and pepper

Heat butter in deep frying pan. Cook parsley, oregano, tarragon and shallots 2 minutes over medium heat; season well.

Pour in vinegar and cook 1 minute over high heat.

Add wine; cook 3 to 4 minutes over high heat.

Pour in chicken stock, bring to boil and continue cooking 3 to 4 minutes. Correct seasoning.

Mix cornstarch with water; stir into sauce and cook 2 to 3 minutes.

Serve this sauce with chicken or veal.

Cook parsley, oregano, tarragon and shallots 2 minutes in hot butter over medium heat; season well.

Pour in chicken stock, bring to boil and continue cooking 3 to 4 minutes. Correct seasoning.

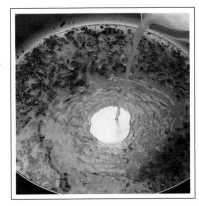

Pour in vinegar, cook 1 minute, then add wine. Cook another 3 to 4 minutes over high heat.

Stir diluted cornstarch into sauce and cook 2 to 3 minutes to thicken.

Curry Sauce

1 SERVING	48 CALORIES	3g CARBOHYDRATE
0g PROTEIN	4g FAT	0.1g FIBER

2 tbsp	(30 ml) butter
2	large onions, finely chopped
3 tbsp	(45 ml) curry powder
2 cups	(500 ml) hot chicken stock
1½ tbsp	(25 ml) cornstarch
3 tbsp	(45 ml) cold water
¼ cup	(50 ml) heavy cream
	dash paprika
	salt and pepper

Heat butter in deep frying pan. When hot, add onions and season with paprika; cook 4 to 5 minutes over medium heat.

Mix in curry powder and cook 3 to 4 minutes over very low heat.

Pour in stock and season well; mix and cook 4 to 5 minutes over medium heat.

Mix cornstarch with water; stir into sauce along with cream. Cook 4 to 5 minutes over low heat.

Serve with a variety of kebabs.

Cook onions seasoned with paprika 4 to 5 minutes over medium heat.
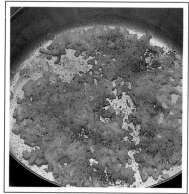

Mix in curry powder and cook 3 to 4 minutes over very low heat.

Pour in stock and season well; mix and cook 4 to 5 minutes over medium heat.
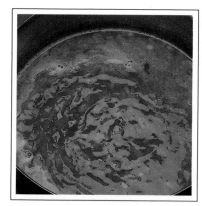

Stir diluted cornstarch and cream into sauce; cook 4 to 5 minutes over low heat.
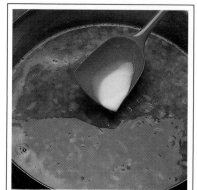

Bourguignonne Sauce

1 SERVING	43 CALORIES	3g CARBOHYDRATE
1g PROTEIN	3g FAT	0.2g FIBER

1 tbsp	(15 ml) vegetable oil
2	shallots, chopped
2	garlic cloves, smashed and chopped
1 tbsp	(15 ml) chopped parsley
1 tbsp	(15 ml) tarragon
1 cup	(250 ml) dry red wine
1	bay leaf
1½ cups	(375 ml) brown sauce, heated
1 cup	(250 ml) diced mushrooms, sautéed
	salt and pepper

Heat oil in deep frying pan. When hot, add shallots, garlic, parsley and tarragon; cook 2 minutes over medium heat.

Add wine, bay leaf and season with pepper; cook 6 to 7 minutes over high heat.

Mix in brown sauce; cook 4 to 5 minutes over medium heat.

Add mushrooms, correct seasoning and cook 2 to 3 minutes.

Serve with beef kebabs. Remember to discard bay leaf before serving.

Cook shallots, garlic, parsley and tarragon in hot oil 2 minutes over medium heat.

Pour in wine, bay leaf and season with pepper; cook 6 to 7 minutes over high heat.

 Mix in brown sauce; cook 4 to 5 minutes over medium heat.

 Add mushrooms, correct seasoning and cook 2 to 3 minutes.

Orange Honey Sauce

1 SERVING	70 CALORIES	13g CARBOHYDRATE
0g PROTEIN	2g FAT	0.2g FIBER

1	onion, finely chopped
1 tbsp	(15 ml) oil
1 cup	(250 ml) orange juice
4 tbsp	(60 ml) honey
1 tbsp	(15 ml) finely chopped fresh ginger
2 tbsp	(30 ml) wine vinegar
	few drops Tabasco sauce

Mix all ingredients together in small saucepan. Bring to boil and continue cooking 2 minutes.

Cool slightly and baste over chicken or pork before broiling.

Peppercorn Sauce

1 SERVING	82 CALORIES	5g CARBOHYDRATE
2g PROTEIN	6g FAT	0.1g FIBER

1 tbsp	(15 ml) butter
1	onion, finely chopped
1 tbsp	(15 ml) chopped parsley
3 tbsp	(45 ml) green peppercorns
½ cup	(125 ml) dry white wine
1 ½ cups	(375 ml) hot white sauce
1 tsp	(5 ml) cumin
	salt and pepper
	dash paprika

Heat butter in saucepan. When hot, add onion and parsley; cook 2 minutes.

Stir in peppercorns and wine; cook 5 minutes over high heat.

Mix in white sauce, cumin and remaining spices; cook 6 to 7 minutes over low heat.

Correct seasoning and serve with almost any kebab.

Tartare Sauce

1 SERVING	99 CALORIES	0g CARBOHYDRATE
0g PROTEIN	11g FAT	0.2g FIBER

1 cup	(250 ml) mayonnaise
3	pickles, finely chopped
24	stuffed green olives, finely chopped
1 tsp	(5 ml) chopped fresh parsley
1 tbsp	(15 ml) capers
¼ tsp	(1 ml) paprika
1 tsp	(5 ml) lemon juice
	salt and pepper

Mix all ingredients together in bowl until well combined. Correct seasoning and chill until serving time.

Stroganoff Sauce

1 SERVING	43 CALORIES	3g CARBOHYDRATE
1g PROTEIN	3g FAT	0.2g FIBER

1 tbsp	(15 ml) olive oil
1	medium onion, finely chopped
¼ lb	(125 g) mushrooms, finely chopped
1 tsp	(5 ml) chopped parsley
½ cup	(125 ml) dry red wine
1 ½ cups	(375 ml) brown sauce, heated
¼ cup	(50 ml) heavy cream
	salt and pepper

Heat oil in deep frying pan. Cook onion 3 minutes over medium heat.

Mix in mushrooms and parsley; cook 2 to 3 minutes.

Pour in wine; cook 4 to 5 minutes over high heat.

Mix in brown sauce, correct seasoning and cook 6 to 7 minutes over medium-low heat.

Stir in cream and finish cooking 2 minutes.

Serve sauce with either beef or chicken.

After onion has **1** cooked 3 minutes, mix in mushrooms and parsley; cook 2 to 3 minutes.

3 Mix in brown sauce, correct seasoning and cook 6 to 7 minutes over medium-low heat.

Pour in wine; **2** cook 4 to 5 minutes over high heat.

4 Stir in cream and finish cooking 2 minutes.

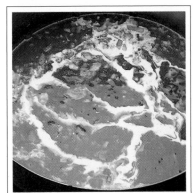

Spicy Kebab Sauce

1 SERVING	61 CALORIES	12g CARBOHYDRATE
1g PROTEIN	1g FAT	0.3g FIBER

2 tbsp	(30 ml) horseradish
1 ½ cups	(375 ml) catsup
½ cup	(125 ml) chili sauce
1 tsp	(5 ml) Worcestershire sauce
	few drops Tabasco sauce
	few drops lime juice
	dash salt

Mix all ingredients together in bowl until well combined. Spread over kebabs and broil as directed in recipe.

Paprika Sauce

1 SERVING	74 CALORIES	4g CARBOHYDRATE
1g PROTEIN	6g FAT	0.2g FIBER

1 cup	(250 ml) chopped onions
2 tbsp	(30 ml) butter
2 tbsp	(30 ml) paprika
½ cup	(125 ml) dry white wine
1 ½ cups	(375 ml) hot white sauce
	few drops Tabasco sauce
	dash salt
	few drops lemon juice

Place onions in small saucepan and pour in water to cover. Bring to boil and continue cooking 2 minutes; drain and set aside.

Heat butter in saucepan. Cook drained onion and paprika 5 to 6 minutes over low heat.

Pour in wine; cook 5 minutes over high heat to reduce liquid by ⅔.

Mix in white sauce and remaining ingredients; cook 6 to 7 minutes over low heat.

Serve sauce with a variety of kebabs.

PASTA

How To Cook Perfect Pasta

We have allowed ¼ livre (125 g) or less of dry pasta per serving, depending on the recipe.

Allow 16 cups (4 l) of water per 1 lb (500 g) of pasta as the water must be able to circulate easily.

To help keep pasta from sticking, add about 1 tbsp (15 ml) of oil or vinegar to the water before adding pasta.

To draw out the pasta's flavor you can add about 1 tsp (5 ml) of salt.

Be sure to bring the water to a full boil before adding pasta and when you do so, stir the noodles well.

During cooking keep the water boiling and stir several times or as often as needed to prevent the pasta from sticking.

One way to check if the pasta is cooked is by biting into a strand or piece and deciding by your preference. The package directions will give you a guidelines for cooking times.

When pasta is 'al dente', stop the cooking process by draining pasta into a colander or large sieve and rinsing with cold water. Shake off excess water and set aside until ready to use. If you need to heat pasta quickly simply rinse with hot water.

For your convenience we have given these measurements in cups, which are equivalent to ¼ lb (125 g) of the pasta listed. All measurements are for dry pasta.

Rotini	1 cup	250 ml
Conch Shells (medium)	1⅓ cups	325 ml
Penne	1¾ cups	425 ml
Fusilli	1¾ cups	425 ml
Macaroni	1 cup	250 ml
Broad Egg Noodles	2¼ cups	550 ml

Last Minute White Spaghetti

(serves 4)

1 SERVING	579 CALORIES	94g CARBOHYDRATE
17g PROTEIN	15g FAT	0.3g FIBER

1 tbsp	(15 ml) white vinegar
1 tsp	(5 ml) salt
1 lb	(500 g) spaghetti
3 tbsp	(45 ml) butter
¼ cup	(50 ml) grated Parmesan cheese
¼ cup	(50 ml) grated mozzarella cheese
¼ cup	(50 ml) grated Gruyère cheese
¼ tsp	(1 ml) celery seed
	white pepper
	dash paprika

Bring 16 cup (4 L) water, vinegar and salt to full boil in large saucepan. Add pasta and stir; cook at full boil uncovered, stirring occasionally. Using package directions as guideline, test pasta several times by biting into strand. When 'al dente', drain into colander reserving ¼ cup (50 ml) of cooking liquid. Rinse pasta with cold water and set aside.

Melt butter in same saucepan. Mix in cheeses and reserved cooking liquid; blend together well.

Add pasta and seasonings; mix well but gently and cook about 2 minutes over medium heat. Stir constantly!

Sprinkle with more paprika and serve immediately.

Four Cheese Sauce and Noodles

(serves 4)

1 SERVING	882 CALORIES	111g CARBOHYDRATE
33g PROTEIN	34g FAT	0.5g FIBER

4 tbsp	(60 ml) butter
4½ tbsp	(65 ml) flour
4 cups	(1 L) hot milk
½ tsp	(2 ml) nutmeg
¼ tsp	(1 ml) ground clove
¼ cup	(50 ml) grated Fontina cheese
¼ cup	(50 ml) crumbled Gorgonzola cheese
¼ cup	(50 ml) diced mozzarella cheese
¼ cup	(50 ml) grated Parmesan cheese
1 lb	(500 g) broad egg noodles, cooked
	salt and pepper

Heat butter in saucepan. Mix in flour and cook 2 to 3 minutes over low heat.

Add half of milk, whisk well and pour in remaining milk. Add seasonings and cook sauce 8 to 10 minutes over low heat.

Stir in cheeses and cook 4 to 5 minutes over low heat. Stir as required.

Serve with noodles.

Basic Tomato Sauce

1 SERVING 4g PROTEIN	154 CALORIES 6g FAT	21g CARBOHYDRATE 2.2g FIBER

2 tbsp	(30 ml) vegetable oil
1 tbsp	(15 ml) melted butter
2	onions, finely chopped
2	garlic cloves, smashed and chopped
12	large tomatoes, peeled and chopped
3	parsley sprigs
1 tsp	(5 ml) oregano
½ tsp	(2 ml) thyme
1	bay leaf
¼ tsp	(1 ml) crushed chillies
5½ oz	(156 ml) can tomato paste
	salt and pepper
	pinch sugar

Heat oil and butter in skillet. Add onions and garlic; mix well, cover and cook 4 to 5 minutes over low heat.

Stir in tomatoes, seasonings, parsley and sugar; continue cooking covered 15 minutes over low heat. Stir occasionally.

Remove cover and stir in tomato paste. Finish cooking 10 to 15 minutes over low heat uncovered.

Force sauce through sieve. This recipe will yield about 4 cups (1 L).

Meat Sauce for Spaghetti

(serves 6 to 8)

1 SERVING 22g PROTEIN	265 CALORIES 13g FAT	15g CARBOHYDRATE 1.7g FIBER

2 tbsp	(30 ml) olive oil
1	onion, chopped
1	carrot, diced small
1	celery stalk, diced small
3	garlic cloves, smashed and chopped
½ lb	(250 g) lean ground pork
½ lb	(250 g) ground beef
¼ lb	(125 g) sausage meat
¼ tsp	(1 ml) crushed chillies
½ tsp	(2 ml) thyme
½ tsp	(2 ml) oregano
¼ tsp	(1 ml) chili powder
¼ tsp	(1 ml) sugar
1	bay leaf
1 cup	(250 ml dry white wine Chardonnay
2	28 oz (796 ml) cans tomatoes, drained and chopped
5 ½ oz	(156 ml) can tomato paste
	salt and pepper

Heat oil in deep skillet. Add onion, carrot, celery and garlic; cover and cook 3 minutes over medium heat.

Add pork, beef and sausage meat; mix well and continue cooking 4 minutes. Do not cover.

Add seasonings, sugar and wine; cook 3 minutes over high heat.

Stir in tomatoes, tomato paste and correct seasoning; bring to boil. Cook sauce, partially covered, about 1 hour over low heat; stir occasionally.

Serve this sauce with spaghetti or use it in a variety of pasta dishes as it is versatile.

1 Cook vegetables and garlic 3 minutes over medium heat. Cover pan.

3 Add seasonings, sugar and wine; cook 3 minutes over high heat.

2 Add pork, beef and sausage meat; mix well and continue cooking 4 minutes uncovered.

4 Stir in tomatoes, tomato paste and correct seasoning; bring to boil. Cook sauce, partially covered, about 1 hour over low heat.

White Sauce

1 SERVING	60 CALORIES	4g CARBOHYDRATE
2g PROTEIN	4g FAT	0g FIBER

4 tbsp	(60 ml) butter
5 tbsp	(75 ml) flour
5 cups	(1.2 L) hot milk
1	onion, studded with 1 clove
¼ tsp	(1 ml) nutmeg
	salt and white pepper

Heat butter in large saucepan. When melted, add flour and mix well. Cook 2 minutes over low heat stirring constantly.

Whisk in half of milk. Incorporate remaining milk and season. Drop in onion, stir in nutmeg and bring to boil.

Cook sauce 8 to 10 minutes over low heat, stirring occasionally. Use this sauce in a variety of pasta recipes.

Spicy Tomato Sauce

1 SERVING	182 CALORIES	15g CARBOHYDRATE
8g PROTEIN	10g FAT	1.5g FIBER

1 tbsp	(15 ml) olive oil
4	slices bacon, diced
1	large onion, finely chopped
2	garlic cloves, smashed and chopped
6	large tomatoes, peeled, seeded and chopped
1	fresh jalapeno pepper, finely chopped
1 tbsp	(15 ml) basil
1 tsp	(5 ml) chili powder
¼ tsp	(1 ml) sugar
¼ cup	(50 ml) grated Parmesan cheese
	salt and pepper

Heat oil in skillet. Cook bacon until crisp then remove, leaving fat in pan. Set bacon aside.

Add onion and garlic to pan; cook 3 to 4 minutes over low heat.

Stir in tomatoes, jalapeno pepper, seasonings and sugar. Cover and cook 20 minutes over low heat; stir occasionally.

Remove cover and continue cooking 15 minutes.

Mix in cheese and bacon. This recipe will yield about 2 cups (500 ml).

Perogies in Sauce

(serves 4)

1 SERVING	465 CALORIES	48g CARBOHYDRATE
21g PROTEIN	21g FAT	2.9g FIBER

2 tbsp	(30 ml) olive oil
1	onion, chopped
½	medium eggplant, cubed
1	zucchini, sliced
½ tsp	(2 ml) oregano
1 lb	(500 g) package perogies, cooked
2 tbsp	(30 ml) butter
28 oz	(796 ml) can tomatoes, drained and chopped
1	garlic clove, smashed and chopped
1 cup	(250 ml) chicken stock, heated
4 tbsp	(60 ml) tomato paste
3 tbsp	(45 ml) ricotta cheese
	salt and pepper

Heat oil in skillet and cook onion 2 minutes over medium heat.

Add eggplant, zucchini, oregano, salt and pepper. Cover and cook 10 to 12 minutes over medium heat stirring occasionally.

Meanwhile brown cooked perogies in 2 tbsp (30 ml) butter. When lightly browned on both sides remove from pan and set aside.

Add tomatoes and garlic to eggplant in skillet; mix very well and pour in chicken stock. Correct seasoning and stir in tomato paste; bring to boil and continue cooking uncovered 8 to 10 minutes.

Mix in cheese and perogies; simmer 2 to 3 minutes or until heated.

After onions have  cooked 3 minutes, mix in curry and continue cooking another 3 minutes. Do not cover.

Add mushrooms  and cook another 3 to 4 minutes.

Pour in chicken stock and season; bring to boil and cook 15 to 18 minutes over medium heat.

 After sauce has thickened, add grapes, banana and water chestnuts and cook 1 minute.

Tortellini with Curry Sauce

(serves 4)

1 SERVING	325 CALORIES	43g CARBOHYDRATE
9g PROTEIN	13g FAT	2.6g FIBER

2 tbsp	(30 ml) oil
2	onions, chopped
2 tbsp	(30 ml) curry powder
½ lb	(250 g) mushrooms, sliced
3 cups	(750 ml) chicken stock, heated
2 tbsp	(30 ml) cornstarch
3 tbsp	(45 ml) cold water
1 cup	(250 ml) seedless green grapes
1	banana, sliced thick
10 oz	(284 ml) can water chestnuts, drained and sliced
½ lb	(250 g) cheese tortellini, cooked
	salt and pepper

Heat oil in skillet. Add onions and cook 3 minutes over medium heat covered.

Mix in curry; continue cooking 3 minutes uncovered.

Add mushrooms and cook another 3 to 4 minutes. Pour in chicken stock and season; bring to boil and cook 15 to 18 minutes over medium heat.

Mix cornstarch with water; stir into sauce and cook 1 minute.

Stir grapes, banana and water chestnuts into mixture; cook 1 minute.

Add tortellini and simmer 3 to 4 minutes.

Yellow Peppers Stuffed with Spaghetti

(serves 4)

1 SERVING	417 CALORIES	70g CARBOHYDRATE
14g PROTEIN	9g FAT	3.6g FIBER

2½ cups	(375 ml) spaghetti, broken into 1 in (2.5 cm) lengths
4	large yellow peppers, blanched 4 minutes
1 tbsp	(15 ml) butter
½ lb	(250 g) mushrooms, diced
2 tbsp	(30 ml) chopped pimento
1¼ cups	(300 ml) tomato sauce, heated
½ cup	(125 ml) ricotta cheese
	salt and pepper

Cook spaghetti al dente. Drain well and set aside.

Using small knife cut tops off peppers and remove white fibers and seeds; set aside on ovenproof platter.

Heat butter in saucepan. Cook mushrooms 3 minutes over medium heat; season well.

Add pimento and spaghetti; mix well and cook 2 minutes.

Stir in tomato sauce and cheese; correct seasoning. Pour into peppers and broil 4 to 5 minutes in oven.

Tortellini in Sauce

(serves 4)

| 1 SERVING | 320 CALORIES | 24g CARBOHYDRATE |
| 11g PROTEIN | 20g FAT | 0.9g FIBER |

3 tbsp	(45 ml) butter
1	onion, chopped
1 tbsp	(15 ml) chopped parsley
1	garlic clove, smashed and chopped
¼ lb	(125 g) mushrooms, diced
1 cup	(250 ml) dry red wine
2 cups	(500 ml) beef stock, heated
2 tbsp	(30 ml) cornstarch
3 tbsp	(45 ml) cold water
½ lb	(250 g) tortellini, cooked
¼ cup	(50 ml) crumbled cooked bacon
½ cup	(125 ml) grated Parmesan cheese
	salt and pepper

Heat butter in skillet. Add onion, parsley and garlic; cook 3 minutes over low heat.

Mix in mushrooms and season; cook 3 to 4 minutes over medium heat.

Pour in wine and cook 4 minutes over high heat. Add beef stock and cook 3 to 4 minutes over medium heat; correct seasoning.

Mix cornstarch with water; stir into sauce and cook 2 minutes.

Add tortellini, simmer 3 to 4 minutes then serve with bacon and cheese.

Fettuccine and Mussels

(serves 4)

| 1 SERVING | 828 CALORIES | 113g CARBOHYDRATE |
| 58g PROTEIN | 16g FAT | 0.7g FIBER |

8½ lb	(4 kg) fresh mussels, scrubbed and bearded
3	shallots, finely chopped
1 tbsp	(15 ml) chopped parsley
2 tbsp	(30 ml) butter
1 cup	(250 ml) dry white wine
2 cups	(500 ml) tomato sauce, heated
1 lb	(500 g) fettuccine, cooked
½ cup	(125 ml) grated Parmesan cheese
	salt and pepper

Place mussels in large pan with shallots, parsley, butter and wine. Cover and bring to boil; cook about 4 to 5 minutes or until shells open.

Remove shells, pouring liquid back into pan. Discard shells and set mussels aside.

Strain cooking liquid through cheesecloth into saucepan. Bring to boil and continue cooking 2 to 3 minutes.

Mix in tomato sauce, season and cook 4 to 5 minutes over medium heat.

Stir mussels and fettuccine into sauce. Cook 3 to 4 minutes over low heat or until heated through.

Serve with cheese.

Fettuccine with Peas

(serves 4)

| 1 SERVING | 737 CALORIES | 103g CARBOHYDRATE |
| 25g PROTEIN | 25g FAT | 1.0g FIBER |

3 tbsp	(45 ml) butter
2 tbsp	(30 ml) grated onion
3 tbsp	(45 ml) flour
2¼ cups	(550 ml) hot milk
¼ tsp	(1 ml) nutmeg
¼ tsp	(1 ml) white pepper
1 lb	(500 g) white fettuccine, cooked
1 cup	(250 ml) snow peas*, blanched
4	slices crisp bacon, finely chopped
½ cup	(125 ml) grated Parmesan cheese
	salt
	few drops Tabasco sauce

Heat butter with onion in saucepan. Mix in flour and cook 2 minutes over low heat, stirring only once.

Pour in half of milk, whisk well and add remaining milk along with seasonings; cook sauce 10 minutes over low heat. Stir at least 2 to 3 times.

Add pasta and peas to sauce; stir and cook 2 to 3 minutes more.

Correct seasoning and garnish portions with bacon and cheese.

* Snow peas are available fresh in the pod. Be careful not to accidently choose the green garden peas which are also sold fresh. After shelling the peas you can save the pods for another recipe such as a stir-fry.

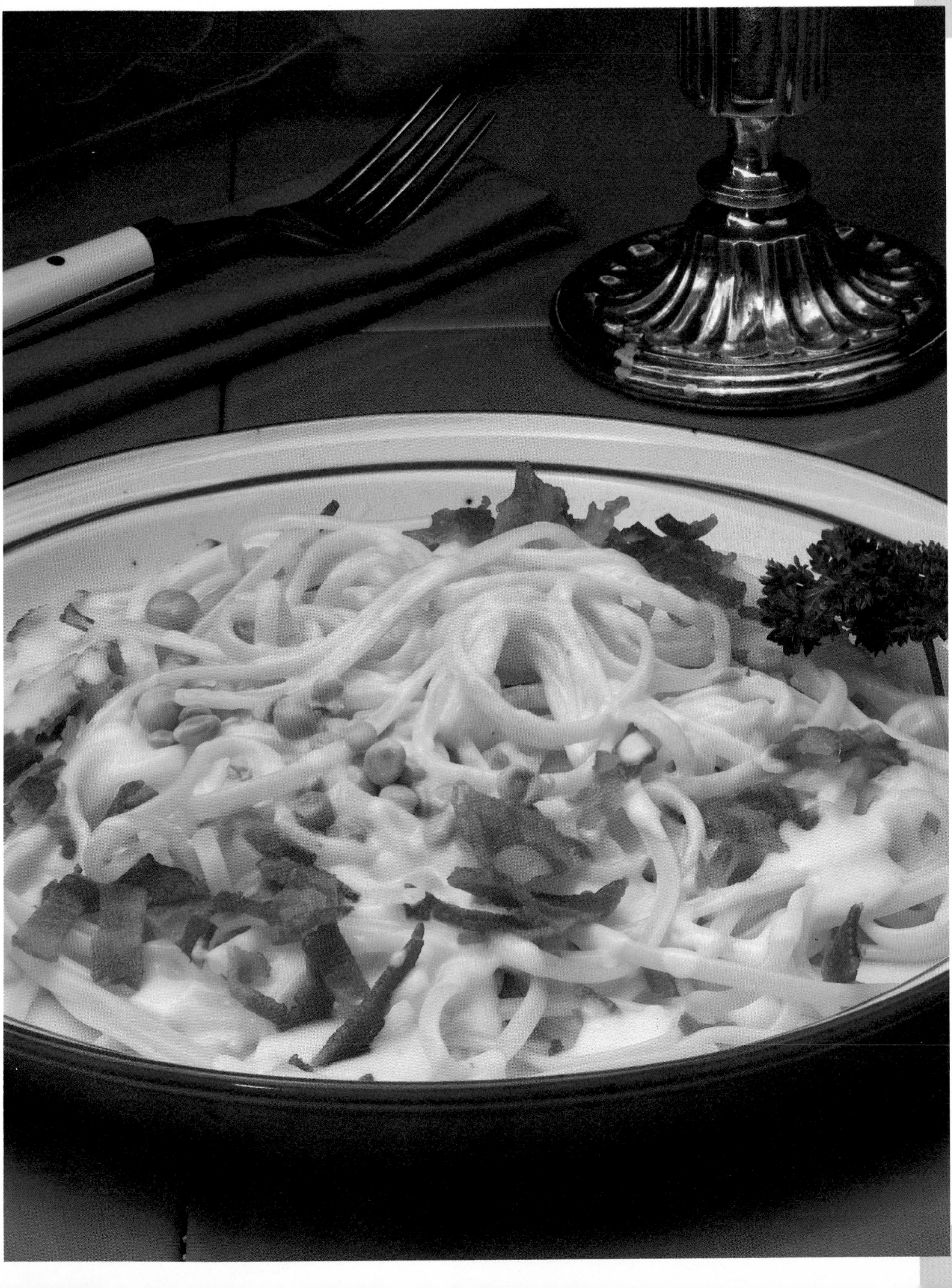

Stuffed Cold Tomatoes

(serves 4)

1 SERVING	216 CALORIES	23g CARBOHYDRATE
4g PROTEIN	12g FAT	3.4g FIBER

8	large tomatoes
3	mint leaves, chopped
2 tbsp	(30 ml) olive oil
1 tsp	(5 ml) wine vinegar
1½ cups	(375 ml) cooked ready-cut macaroni
3 tbsp	(45 ml) mustard vinaigrette or substitute
1 tbsp	(15 ml) chopped parsley
1	green pepper, finely chopped
2 tbsp	(30 ml) pickled sweet pimento
	salt and pepper

Using sharp knife and spoon, hollow tomatoes. Discard insides and set shells aside.

Mix chopped mint, oil and vinegar together. Season well and sprinkle in tomatoes; let stand 15 minutes.

Mix macaroni with remaining ingredients; let stand 15 minutes.

Fill tomatoes with macaroni mixture, chill 15 minutes, and serve.

Meaty Macaroni and Cheese

(serves 4)

1 SERVING	826 CALORIES	88g CARBOHYDRATE
60g PROTEIN	26g FAT	2.0g FIBER

2 tbsp	(30 ml) olive oil
1	onion, finely chopped
1	garlic clove, smashed and chopped
½ tsp	(2 ml) oregano
1 tbsp	(15 ml) chopped parsley
½ lb	(250 g) ground beef
½ lb	(250 g) lean ground pork
1½	28 oz (796 ml) cans tomatoes, drained and chopped
¾ lb	(375 g) macaroni, cooked
¾ lb	(375 g) ricotta cheese
	salt and pepper

Heat oil in skillet. Add onion and cook 3 minutes over low heat.

Stir in garlic, seasonings and meats; cook 5 to 6 minutes over medium heat stirring often.

Mix in tomatoes and correct seasoning. Continue cooking 10 to 12 minutes over low heat.

Add macaroni and cheese; cook 4 to 5 minutes over low heat and serve.

Seafood Macaroni

(serves 4)

1 SERVING	795 CALORIES	112g CARBOHYDRATE
53g PROTEIN	15g FAT	5.1g FIBER

5	large tomatoes, cut in 2 and seeded
1 tbsp	(15 ml) olive oil
1	large onion, finely chopped
½ tsp	(2 ml) basil
½ tsp	(2 ml) tarragon
½ tsp	(2 ml) chopped parsley
1 lb	(500 g) small cooked shrimp
1 lb	(500 g) macaroni, cooked
1 cup	(250 ml) ricotta cheese
	pinch sugar
	salt and pepper

Purée tomatoes in blender for 3 minutes.

Heat oil in large frying pan. Cook onion 3 minutes over low heat.

Add basil, tarragon, parsley, sugar and tomatoes; season well. Cook 25 to 30 minutes over low heat.

Stir in shrimp, macaroni and cheese; cook 3 minutes or until heated through.

Serve.

Garnished Penne

(serves 4)

1 SERVING	623 CALORIES	90g CARBOHYDRATE
23g PROTEIN	19g FAT	0.5g FIBER

2 tbsp	(30 ml) butter
¼ cup	(50 ml) Monterey Jack or cheddar, crumbled or grated
½ cup	(125 ml) grated Parmesan cheese
1 lb	(500 g) penne, cooked and still hot
12	thin slices salami, in julienne
	salt and pepper
	chopped parsley

Heat butter in large saucepan over medium-low heat. Stir in cheeses and cook 2 minutes over low heat. Mix to avoid sticking.

Add hot penne and season generously. Mix well and continue cooking 2 to 3 minutes over low heat.

Stir in salami, garnish with chopped parsley and serve.

Penne Vegetable Salad

(serves 4)

1 SERVING	591 CALORIES	95g CARBOHYDRATE
31g PROTEIN	43g FAT	1.7g FIBER

1 lb	(500 g) penne, cooked
1	yellow pepper, in julienne
½	zucchini, in julienne and blanched
4	slices cooked ham, in julienne
1	large tomato, cored and in wedges
½ cup	(125 ml) pitted black olives
1 tbsp	(15 ml) chopped parsley
½ tsp	(2 ml) chopped fresh oregano
3	mint leaves, chopped
1	egg yolk
2 tbsp	(30 ml) catsup
3 tbsp	(45 ml) wine vinegar
½ cup	(125 ml) olive oil
½ cup	(125 ml) grated Parmesan cheese
1 tbsp	(15 ml) chopped jalapeno peppers
	salt and pepper

In large serving bowl, toss together penne, yellow pepper, zucchini, ham, tomato, olives, parsley, oregano and mint.

In another bowl mix egg yolk with catsup. Incorporate vinegar then slowly add oil while mixing constantly.

Add remaining ingredients and poor over salad. Toss and serve.

Linguine with Artichoke Hearts

(serves 4)

1 SERVING	707 CALORIES	195g CARBOHYDRATE
20g PROTEIN	23g FAT	1.3g FIBER

5 tbsp	(75 ml) butter
4½ tbsp	(65 ml) flour
2 cups	(500 ml) hot chicken stock
8	artichoke hearts, quartered
1	garlic clove, smashed and chopped
½ cup	(125 ml) stuffed green olives, halved
1 tbsp	(15 ml) chopped parsley
¼ cup	(50 ml) dry white wine Chardonnay
1 lb	(500 g) linguine, cooked
½ cup	(125 ml) grated Parmesan cheese
	salt and pepper
	dash paprika

Heat 4 tbsp (60 ml) butter in saucepan. Mix in flour and cook 2 minutes over low heat while stirring.

Pour in chicken stock, mix very well and season generously. Cook 8 to 10 minutes over low heat.

Meanwhile, heat remaining butter in frying pan. Cook artichoke hearts, garlic, olives and parsley 2 to 3 minutes over medium heat. Season well.

Incorporate white wine and continue cooking mixture 2 to 3 minutes.

Add artichoke mixture to sauce and mix well. Pour over pasta and sprinkle with cheese and paprika before serving.

Meaty Lasagne

(serves 6)

1 SERVING	785 CALORIES	85g CARBOHYDRATE
64g PROTEIN	21g FAT	2.4g FIBER

1½ cups	(375 ml) cottage cheese
¼ tsp	(1 ml) allspice
½ tsp	(2 ml) oregano
1 tbsp	(15 ml) chopped lemon rind
½ cup	(125 ml) grated Parmesan cheese
2 tbsp	(30 ml) vegetable oil
2	onions, chopped
1	celery stalk, chopped
2	garlic cloves, smashed and chopped
1 lb	(500 g) ground beef
½ lb	(250 g) ground veal
1 lb	(500 g) mushrooms, chopped
1 lb	(500 g) lasagne, cooked
1¼ cups	(300 ml) grated mozzarella cheese
4 cups	(1 L) hot tomato sauce
	salt and pepper

Preheat oven to 375°F (190°C). Grease lasagne dish.

Mix cottage cheese, allspice, oregano, lemon rind and Parmesan cheese together in bowl; set aside.

Heat oil in large skillet; cook onions, celery and garlic 3 to 4 minutes over medium heat.

Add meats, mix well and brown 5 to 6 minutes; season well. Mix in mushrooms and finish cooking 3 to 4 minutes over high heat. Correct seasoning and remove from stove.

Dividing ingredients equally build lasagne with layers of pasta, meat, cottage cheese, mozzarella and tomato sauce. End with a layer of pasta then cover with sauce and remaining mozzarella.

Bake 50 minutes in oven.

Rolling Lasagne

(serves 4)

1 SERVING	949 CALORIES	57g CARBOHYDRATE
70g PROTEIN	49g FAT	0.9g FIBER

2 tbsp	(30 ml) vegetable oil
1	small onion, finely chopped
¼ tsp	(1 ml) thyme
1 tsp	(5 ml) oregano
1 tbsp	(15 ml) chopped parsley
¼ tsp	(1 ml) ground clove
1 lb	(500 g) ground veal
3	slices ham, finely chopped
¼ cup	(50 ml) hot chicken stock
1 cup	(250 ml) cooked spinach, chopped
3 oz	(90 g) diced mozzarella cheese
1	beaten egg
8	strips lasagne, cooked
4 cups	(1 L) hot white sauce
1 cup	(250 ml) grated Gruyère cheese
	salt and pepper
	paprika to taste

Preheat oven to 375°F (190°C).

Heat oil in large frying pan. Add onion, thyme, oregano, parsley and clove; cover and cook 3 minutes.

Stir in veal and ham; season and cook 3 minutes uncovered.

Add chicken stock and spinach; cook 3 to 4 minutes. Stir in mozzarella and cook 2 to 3 minutes while mixing. Remove pan from heat and cool.

Add egg to bind stuffing. Lay lasagne strips flat and sprinkle with paprika. Spread stuffing over full length of strips and roll.

Place rolls in baking dish and cover with white sauce; top with cheese. Bake 20 minutes in oven. Serve with a vegetable garnish or salad.

Lay lasagne strips flat and sprinkle with paprika for extra taste.

Spread stuffing over full length of each strip then roll.

 Place rolls in baking dish and cover with white sauce.

 Top with cheese and bake 20 minutes in oven.

Vegetable Lasagne

(serves 6)

1 SERVING	666 CALORIES	81g CARBOHYDRATE
27g PROTEIN	26g FAT	4.7g FIBER

½ cup	(125 ml) grated Parmesan cheese
½ cup	(125 ml) grated Gruyère cheese
½ cup	(125 ml) grated Romano cheese
3 tbsp	(45 ml) butter
1	red onion, finely diced
1	celery stalk, finely diced
1	small zucchini, diced
½	small cauliflower, diced
1	yellow pepper, diced
1	small eggplant, finely diced
1 tbsp	(15 ml) chopped parsley
1 tbsp	(15 ml) grated lemon rind
½ tsp	(2 ml) nutmeg and ground clove
2	garlic cloves, smashed and chopped
¼ cup	(50 ml) chicken stock, heated
1 lb	(500 g) lasagne, cooked
6	tomatoes, thinly sliced
3 cups	(750 ml) thin white sauce, heated
½ cup	(125 ml) tomato sauce, heated
	salt and pepper
	sliced mozzarella for topping
	paprika to taste

Preheat oven to 375°F (190°C). Grease lasagne dish.

Mix grated cheeses together; set aside.

Heat butter in large skillet; cook onion and celery 4 minutes over low heat.

Add remaining vegetables (except tomatoes), parsley, lemon rind, seasonings, garlic and chicken stock. Mix well, cover and cook 10 to 12 minutes over low heat.

Dividing ingredients equally, build lasagne with layers of pasta, vegetables, tomatoes, grated cheeses and white sauce. End with a layer of pasta then cover with tomato sauce and mozzarella cheese; sprinkle with paprika.

Place lasagne dish on cookie sheet and bake about 50 minutes.

Cook vegetables  (except tomatoes), seasonings, garlic and chicken stock in large skillet for 10 to 12 minutes. Be sure to cover pan and keep heat low.

When building  the lasagne try to spread layers evenly.

 After the layers of lasagne, vegetables, tomatoes and grated cheeses, top with white sauce.

 End with a layer of pasta then cover with tomato sauce and mozzarella cheese; sprinkle with paprika.

Fusilli, Broccoli and Cheese

(serves 4)

1 SERVING	892 CALORIES	101g CARBOHYDRATE
32g PROTEIN	40g FAT	1.1g FIBER

2	small heads broccoli, in flowerets
1½ cups	(375 ml) cold light cream
½ lb	(250 g) Gorgonzola cheese, crumbled
1 tbsp	(15 ml) butter
1 tbsp	(15 ml) chopped parsley
1 lb	(500 g) fusilli, cooked
	few drops lemon juice
	salt and pepper

Cook broccoli in boiling salted water for 3 to 4 minutes. Drain and set aside. Sprinkle with lemon juice.

Pour cream into saucepan and bring to boiling point. Add cheese and butter; mix very well and season.

Cook 4 to 5 minutes over low heat to melt cheese. Stir occasionally.

Stir in broccoli, parsley and lemon juice; simmer 1 to 2 minutes then serve with pasta.

Fusilli and Chicken Livers

(serves 4)

1 SERVING	648 CALORIES	87g CARBOHYDRATE
39g PROTEIN	16g FAT	1.8g FIBER

1 tbsp	(15 ml) oil
1 lb	(500 g) chicken livers, cut in 2
2 tbsp	(30 ml) butter
1	onion, finely chopped
½ lb	(250 g) mushrooms, diced
1	red pepper, diced
½ cup	(125 ml) dry red wine
1 cup	(250 ml) tomato sauce, heated
1 cup	(250 ml) beef stock, heated
¼ tsp	(1 ml) thyme
½ tsp	(2 ml) basil
1 tsp	(5 ml) cornstarch
2 tbsp	(30 ml) cold water
¾ lb	(375 g) fusilli, cooked and still hot
	salt and pepper

Heat oil in frying pan and cook livers 3 minutes each side; season well. Remove and set aside.

Add butter, onion and mushrooms to pan; cook 3 minutes over medium heat. Add red pepper and cook 2 minutes; season well.

Pour in wine and cook 3 minutes over high heat. Mix in tomato sauce, beef stock and seasonings; cook 2 minutes.

Mix cornstarch with water; stir into sauce and cook 1 minute. Add livers, simmer 5 minutes then pour over hot fusilli.

Eggplant and Conch Shells

(serves 4)

1 SERVING	567 CALORIES	92g CARBOHYDRATE
16g PROTEIN	15g FAT	2.8g FIBER

2	medium eggplants
3 tbsp	(45 ml) olive oil
1	garlic clove, smashed and chopped
1 tbsp	(15 ml) chopped parsley
1 tsp	(5 ml) marjoram
2 cups	(500 ml) spicy tomato sauce, heated
¾ lb	(375 g) medium conch shells, cooked
½ cup	(125 ml) marinated pitted black olives, sliced
	salt and pepper

Preheat oven to 375°F (190°C).

Cut eggplants in half lengthwise. Score flesh and brush with 2 tbsp (30 ml) oil. Bake 50 minutes in oven.

When cooked, remove and chop flesh.

Heat remaining oil in skillet and cook garlic 1 minute. Add eggplant and seasonings; mix and cook 3 to 4 minutes over high heat.

Pour in tomato sauce, mix well and simmer 5 minutes over low heat.

Stir in conch shells and olives; simmer 2 to 3 minutes over low heat.

Rotini
with Mushrooms

(serves 4)

1 SERVING	623 CALORIES	77g CARBOHYDRATE
18g PROTEIN	27g FAT	0.8g FIBER

2 tbsp	(30 ml) olive oil
2 cups	(500 ml) quartered mushrooms
2 tbsp	(30 ml) capers
1 tsp	(5 ml) chopped fresh parsley
½ tsp	(2 ml) oregano
½ cup	(125 ml) dry red wine Valpolicella
1½ cups	(375 ml) hot light cream
2 tbsp	(30 ml) tomato paste
2	green onions, chopped
¾ lb	(375 g) rotini, cooked
¼ cup	(375 g) grated Parmesan cheese
	salt and pepper

Heat oil in saucepan. Add mushrooms, capers, parsley, oregano, salt and pepper; cook 3 to 4 minutes over medium heat.

Pour in red wine and cook 3 to 4 minutes over high heat.

Add cream and mix well. Stir in tomato paste and onions; cook 3 to 4 minutes over low heat.

Correct seasoning and serve sauce with pasta. Sprinkle with cheese before serving.

86

Egg Noodles and Anchovies

(serves 4)

1 SERVING	677 CALORIES	80g CARBOHYDRATE
24g PROTEIN	29g FAT	2.3g FIBER

5	large tomatoes, peeled
2 tbsp	(30 ml) olive oil
1	garlic clove, smashed and chopped
3	fresh basil leaves, chopped
1	small jalapeno pepper, in 2 pieces
4	anchovy filets, chopped
1 cup	(250 ml) marinated black olives, pitted
3 tbsp	(45 ml) capers
1 cup	(250 ml) grated Emmentaler cheese
¾ lb	(375 g) extra-broad egg noodles, cooked
	salt and pepper

Purée tomatoes in blender; set aside.

Heat oil in skillet and cook garlic and basil 1 minute over medium heat.

Add tomatoes and pieces of jalapeno; mix well and stir in anchovies. Bring to boil and cook 18 to 20 minutes over low heat. During cooking, taste sauce occasionally; remove jalapeno pieces when they have imparted enough flavour.

Add remaining ingredients and mix well. Cook 3 to 4 minutes before serving.

Purée tomatoes in blender.

Add tomatoes and pieces of jalapeno to cooking garlic and basil leaves.
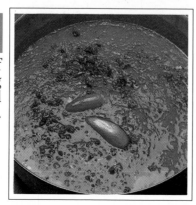

Mix well and stir in anchovies. Bring sauce to boil and cook 18 to 20 minutes over low heat.

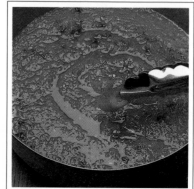
During cooking, taste sauce occasionally and when pleased with taste remove jalapeno pieces.

Spinach Egg Noodles Stroganoff

(serves 4)

1 SERVING 59g PROTEIN	781 CALORIES 25g FAT	80g CARBOHYDRATE 1.3g FIBER

1 tbsp	(15 ml) vegetable oil
1½ lb	(750 g) sirloin steak, cut in 1 in (2.5 cm) strips
2 tbsp	(30 ml) melted butter
2	shallots, chopped
1	onion, thinly sliced
½ lb	(250 g) mushrooms, diced
1 tbsp	(15 ml) chopped parsley
¼ tsp	(1 ml) thyme
1 cup	(250 ml) dry red wine Valpolicella
2 cups	(500 ml) beef stock, heated
1½ tbsp	(25 ml) cornstarch
3 tbsp	(45 ml) cold water
¾ lb	(375 g) broad spinach egg noodles, cooked
½ cup	(125 ml) ricotta cheese
	salt and pepper

Heat oil in frying pan. Add meat and cook 2 minutes over medium-high heat. Turn over, season and cook 1 more minute. Remove meat from pan.

Add butter, shallots and onion; cook 3 minutes over low heat.

Add mushrooms, parsley and thyme; cook 3 minutes over medium heat.

Correct seasoning and add wine; cook 3 minutes over high heat. Stir in beef stock; cook 3 minutes over low heat.

Mix cornstarch with water; stir into sauce and cook about 2 minutes.

Replace meat in sauce, fold in noodles and simmer 2 minutes. Stir in cheese and serve.

Continental Egg Noodles

(serves 4)

1 SERVING 16g PROTEIN	765 CALORIES 21g FAT	128g CARBOHYDRATE 1.7g FIBER

3 tbsp	(45 ml) butter
2	onions, finely chopped
2	green onions, finely chopped
3 tbsp	(45 ml) curry powder
1 tsp	(5 ml) cumin
3 cups	(750 ml) chicken stock, heated
2 tbsp	(30 ml) cornstarch
3 tbsp	(45 ml) cold water
½ cup	(125 ml) golden raisins
½ cup	(125 ml) grated coconut
1 lb	(500 g) broad egg noodles, cooked
½ cup	(125 ml) plain yogurt
	salt and pepper
	sesame seeds

Heat butter in large skillet. Add both onions and cook 3 to 4 minutes over low heat. Stir in curry and cumin; continue cooking 3 to 4 minutes.

Add chicken stock, season and bring to boil. Cook 15 minutes over low heat.

Mix cornstarch with water; stir into sauce and cook 1 minute.

Add raisins, coconut and noodles; simmer 2 to 3 minutes.

Stir in yogurt and top with sesame seeds.

Vermicelli and Spinach

(serves 4)

1 SERVING	701 CALORIES	110g CARBOHYDRATE
27g PROTEIN	17g FAT	1.9g FIBER

1 lb	(500 g) spinach leaves
2 tbsp	(30 ml) olive oil
2	garlic cloves, smashed and chopped
3 cups	(750 ml) tomato sauce, heated
1 lb	(500 g) vermicelli, cooked
1 cup	(250 ml) grated Parmesan cheese
	salt and pepper

Wash spinach very well. Cool about 3 to 4 minutes in salted boiling water; cover pan.

Drain spinach, shape into balls and squeeze out all excess water. Chop and set aside.

Heat oil in skillet. When hot, add garlic and spinach; cook 3 minutes over high heat.

Add tomato sauce, vermicelli, salt and pepper; simmer 2 to 3 minutes over medium-low heat.

Serve with cheese.

Vermicelli, Bacon and Peas

(serves 4)

1 SERVING	489 CALORIES	83g CARBOHYDRATE
19g PROTEIN	9g FAT	5.8g FIBER

2 tbsp	(30 ml) butter
1	Spanish onion, chopped
½ tsp	(2 ml) oregano
½ tsp	(2 ml) paprika
4	slices back bacon, in strips
¼ cup	(50 ml) dry red wine
1½ cups	(375 ml) beef stock, heated
1½ tbsp	(25 ml) cornstarch
3 tbsp	(45 ml) cold water
1½ cups	(375 ml) frozen green peas, cooked
¾ lb	(375 g) vermicelli, cooked
¼ cup	(125 ml) grated Parmesan cheese
	salt and pepper

Heat butter in skillet; cook onion and seasonings 8 to 10 minutes over low heat.

Add bacon and cook 3 to 4 minutes. Stir in wine and cook 3 minutes over high heat.

Mix in beef stock and cook 5 to 6 minutes over medium heat. Mix cornstarch with water; stir into sauce and cook 1 minute.

Add peas and vermicelli; mix well and simmer 3 minutes. Stir in cheese and serve.

Cook onion and seasonings 8 to 10 minutes over low heat.

Add bacon and cook 3 to 4 minutes. Pour in wine, stir and cook 3 minutes over high heat.

Stir diluted cornstarch into sauce and cook 1 minute to thicken.

Add peas and vermicelli; mix well and simmer 3 minutes. Stir in cheese before serving.

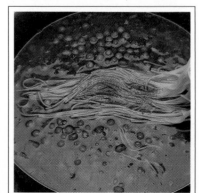

Layered Gnocchi

(serves 4)

1 SERVING	488 CALORIES	42g CARBOHYDRATE
26g PROTEIN	24g FAT	0.3g FIBER

½ cup	(125 ml) ricotta cheese
2	eggs
1 cup	(250 ml) grated Parmesan cheese
1½ cups	(375 ml) sifted flour
1 cup	(250 ml) grated Gruyère cheese
1½ cups	(375 ml) thin white sauce, heated
1 cup	(250 ml) tomato sauce, heated
1 tbsp	(15 ml) chopped parsley
	salt and pepper
	paprika

Preheat oven to 375°F (190°C).

Place ricotta, eggs, Parmesan, salt and pepper in blender; mix 1 minute.

Add flour and mix 1 minute; transfer dough to bowl, cover and refrigerate 1 hour.

Bring plenty of salted water to boiling point. Drop in small pieces of dough and cook 8 minutes. Keep water at boiling point and when cooked, remove with slotted spoon and drain on paper towels. Depending on the size of pan you may have to cook gnocchi in two batches.

Place half of gnocchi in lightly greased baking dish. Add half of Gruyère, half of white sauce and paprika.

Pour in half of tomato sauce and finish with remaining gnocchi, cheese, parsley and sauces.

Bake 30 to 35 minutes in oven.

After dough has been chilled, drop small pieces into hot water and cook 8 minutes. Do not crowd.

Place half of gnocchi in lightly greased baking dish. Add half of Gruyère, half of white sauce and paprika.

Pour in half of tomato sauce.

Finish with remaining gnocchi, cheese, parsley and sauces.

Potato Gnocchi

(serves 4)

1 SERVING	400 CALORIES	42g CARBOHYDRATE
13g PROTEIN	20g FAT	1.0g FIBER

1 cup	(250 ml) flour
2 cups	(500 ml) cooked riced potatoes
4 tbsp	(60 ml) butter
½ cup	(125 ml) grated mozzarella cheese
1½ cups	(375 ml) tomato sauce, heated
½ cup	(125 ml) ricotta cheese
	salt and white pepper
	pinch nutmeg

Place flour in bowl and form well in center. Add potatoes, nutmeg and 3 tbsp (45 ml) butter; pinch dough to incorporate.

Season and remove dough from bowl. Place on counter and knead with the heel of your hand until smooth.

Shape dough into ball and cut into 4 quarters. Roll each quarter into a cylindrical shape with a diameter of about 1 in (2.5 cm). Slice into ½ in (1.2 cm) pieces.

Cook in salted simmering water for about 5 minutes. Monitor heat to keep water simmering without breaking into a boil.

When cooked, gnocchi should rise to the surface. Remove with slotted spoon and set aside to drain on paper towel.

Preheat oven to 375°F (190°C).

With remaining butter grease large baking dish.

Season mozzarella with salt and pepper. Mix ricotta cheese with tomato sauce over low heat for 1 minute.

Layer gnocchi, mozzarella and sauce in baking dish. Bake 12 minutes.

Change oven setting to broil and continue cooking 4 minutes. Serve.

BUDGET COOKING

BUDGET COOKING

Economical cooking should not imply that you're getting the bottom of the barrel nor should it be an indication of a meal with little taste, variety or nutrition. But rather, inexpensive eating should simply mean that you're getting your money's worth and making the most of what you buy. As you are probably well aware, there are many ways of literally saving cash such as using coupons, taking advantage of in-store sales or just generally 'shopping around'. But the best rule of thumb I can offer you is to never settle for poor quality and pay for it! Treat food shopping as you would any other — if the goods are damaged or not up to par, the price should be adjusted accordingly. If on Tuesday the red peppers are a sorry lot then substitute them for another vegetable that is fresh and worth your money — in other words be ready to compromise! Aside from being flexible, be prepared to spend a little extra time in the kitchen as some foods like inexpensive cuts of meat may need marinating or longer cooking times to bring out the best flavor and tenderness. And lastly, think of your freezer as you would your best friend. Let's get started...

Corned Beef and Cabbage

(serves 4)

1 SERVING	1777 CALORIES	54g CARBOHYDRATE
73g PROTEIN	141g FAT	6.3g FIBER

4 lb	(1.8 kg) corned beef brisket
3	cloves
1	bay leaf
3	parsley sprigs
½ tsp	(2 ml) thyme
1	large cabbage, cut in 4
8	carrots, pared
4	large potatoes, peeled and cut in half
2	leeks, cut in 4 lengthwise to within 1 in (2.5 cm) of base, washed
	salt and pepper

Place brisket in large saucepan and pour in enough cold water to cover beef by 3 in (7.5 cm). Bring to boil, then skim.

Add cloves, bay leaf, parsley and thyme; partially cover and cook 3 hours over low heat. Skim if necessary.

Meanwhile, blanch cabbage and carrots in salted boiling water about 10 minutes. Drain well.

Add blanched vegetables, potatoes and leeks to beef. Continue cooking 1 hour partially covered.

To serve, remove beef and vegetables from liquid and arrange on serving platter. Moisten beef with a little bit of cooking liquid, slice and serve.

Boiled Beef

(serves 4)

1 SERVING	486 CALORIES	7g CARBOHYDRATE
56g PROTEIN	26g FAT	1.5g FIBER

4 lb	(1.8 kg) cross-rib roast, tied
2	celery stalks, cut in ½
2	leeks, cut in 4 lengthwise to within 1 in (2.5 cm) of base, washed
1	Spanish onion, cut in 4
2	garlic cloves, peeled and whole
4	cloves
½ tsp	(2 ml) allspice
4	parsley sprigs
2	bay leaves
	salt and pepper

Place all ingredients in large saucepan and pour in enough cold water to cover; bring to boil.

Skim then continue cooking 4 hours over low heat; partially cover. Serve with horseradish sauce.

Horseradish Sauce

1 SERVING	51 CALORIES	5g CARBOHYDRATE
1g PROTEIN	3g FAT	0.5g FIBER

4 tbsp	(60 ml) horseradish
2 tbsp	(30 ml) sour cream
1 tbsp	(15 ml) breadcrumbs
⅓ cup	(75 ml) whipped heavy cream
	few drops Tabasco sauce
	fresh ground pepper

Mix horseradish, sour cream and breadcrumbs together.

Add remaining ingredients and season generously. Serve with boiled beef.

Pot Roast

(serves 4)

1 SERVING	488 CALORIES	21g CARBOHYDRATE
56g PROTEIN	20g FAT	3.0g FIBER

2 tbsp	(30 ml) vegetable oil
3 lb	(1.4 kg) sirloin tip roast
5	onions, peeled, cut in 4
2 cups	(500 ml) dry red wine
2 cups	(500 ml) tomato sauce, heated
1	garlic clove, smashed and chopped
½ tsp	(2 ml) thyme
½ tsp	(2 ml) basil
½ tsp	(2 ml) allspice
	salt and pepper

Preheat oven to 350°F (180°C).

Heat oil in large ovenproof casserole. Sear beef 6 to 8 minutes over medium-high heat on all sides; season well.

Add onions and continue cooking 6 to 8 minutes over medium heat.

Pour in wine and tomato sauce. Add garlic, seasonings and bring to boil.

Cover and cook 2½ hours in oven.

Serve with additional vegetables if desired.

Sear beef 6 to 8 minutes over medium-high heat on all sides; season well.

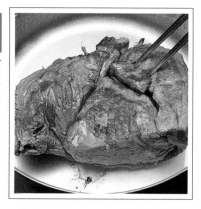

Add onions and continue cooking 6 to 8 minutes over medium heat.

Pour in wine.

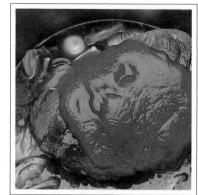

Pour in tomato sauce. Add garlic, seasonings and bring to boil. Finish cooking 2½ hours in oven.

Beef Stew

(serves 4)

1 SERVING 36g PROTEIN	513 CALORIES 25g FAT	36g CARBOHYDRATE 3.0g FIBER

2 tbsp	(30 ml) vegetable oil
2 lb	(900 g) stewing beef, cubed
½ tsp	(2 ml) chili powder
4 tbsp	(60 ml) flour
1 tbsp	(15 ml) butter
1	garlic clove, smashed and chopped
1	onion, coarsely chopped
1	celery stalk, diced
¼ tsp	(1 ml) thyme
1	clove
½ tsp	(2 ml) tarragon
½ tsp	(2 ml) basil
28 oz	(796 ml) can tomatoes
2½ cups	(625 ml) beef stock, heated
2 tbsp	(30 ml) tomato paste
2	large potatoes, peeled and cubed
2	large carrots, pared and cubed
	salt and pepper

Preheat oven to 350°F (180°C).

Heat oil in ovenproof casserole. Sear meat (in two batches) 3 minutes over medium-high heat. Turn pieces over and add chili powder, salt and pepper; finish searing 3 minutes.

With all meat in casserole sprinkle in flour. Mix well and cook 2 to 3 minutes over medium heat.

Remove meat and set aside.

Add butter to casserole. Cook garlic, onion, celery and seasonings 3 to 4 minutes over medium heat.

Pour in tomatoes with juice and correct seasoning. Replace meat and mix well.

Add beef stock, mix and stir in tomato paste; cover and bring to boil. Finish cooking 2 hours in oven.

1 hour before beef is cooked, add vegetables to casserole, forty minutes later, remove cover.

Serve stew with garlic bread.

Sear meat (in two batches) 3 minutes over medium-high heat. Turn pieces over and add chili powder, salt and pepper; finish searing 3 minutes.

Cook garlic, onion, celery and seasonings 3 to 4 minutes over medium heat.

With all meat in casserole sprinkle in flour. Mix well and cook 2 to 3 minutes over medium heat.

Pour in tomatoes with juice and correct seasoning.

Stir-fry meat and  garlic for 2 minutes then pour in soya sauce. Mix well to coat meat strips then remove.

Add onions and cucumbers to pan; cook 2 minutes over high heat. Season with pepper.

 Add yellow pepper and pea pods; continue cooking 2 to 3 minutes over high heat stirring frequently.

 Replace meat in pan along with sprouts; simmer 2 to 3 minutes over medium-low heat before serving.

Beef Stir-Fry

(serves 4)

1 SERVING	410 CALORIES	11g CARBOHYDRATE
51g PROTEIN	18g FAT	2.2g FIBER

2 tbsp	(30 ml) vegetable oil
2 lb	(900 g) strip loin steak, cut in strips
1	garlic clove, smashed and chopped
2 tbsp	(30 ml) soya sauce
4	green onions, in 2.5 cm lengths
1	red onion, cut in half and sliced
2	dill cucumbers, sliced
1	yellow pepper, sliced
7 oz	(200 g) snow peas, ends trimmed
1 cup	(250 ml) bean sprouts
	salt and pepper

Heat oil in large frying pan. When hot, add meat and garlic; stir-fry 2 minutes.

Season and pour in soya sauce; mix well and remove meat from pan.

Add onions and cucumbers to pan; cook 2 minutes over high heat. Season with pepper.

Add yellow pepper and snow peas; continue cooking 2 to 3 minutes over high heat stirring frequently.

Replace meat in pan along with sprouts; simmer 2 to 3 minutes over medium-low heat before serving.

Chuck Roast with Vegetables

(serves 4)

1 SERVING	749 CALORIES	24g CARBOHYDRATE
71g PROTEIN	41g FAT	3.7g FIBER

2 tbsp	(30 ml) vegetable oil
4-5 lb	(1.8-2.3 kg) chuck short rib roast, tied
3	onions, peeled, cut in 4
1	bay leaf
¼ tsp	(1 ml) thyme
¼ tsp	(1 ml) basil
1½ cups	(375 ml) beer
1½ cups	(375 ml) brown sauce
4	carrots, pared
4	leeks, cut in 4 lengthwise to within 1 in (2.5 cm) of base, washed
1 tbsp	(15 ml) cornstarch
3 tbsp	(45 ml) cold water
	salt and pepper

Preheat oven to 350°F (180°C).

Heat oil in ovenproof casserole. Sear meat 8 to 10 minutes on all sides.

Add onions, bay leaf and seasonings; continue cooking 4 to 5 minutes.

Pour in beer and bring to boil. Add brown sauce and bring to boil again.

Cover and cook 2½ hours in oven.

About 1 hour before roast is cooked, add carrots to casserole. And 20 minutes later, add leeks.

Arrange beef and vegetables on serving platter.

Place casserole over medium-high heat and bring liquid to boil. Mix cornstarch with water; stir into sauce and cook 3 to 4 minutes over medium heat to thicken.

Correct seasoning and serve sauce with beef and vegetables.

Mock Pepper Steak

(serves 4)

1 SERVING	387 CALORIES	12g CARBOHYDRATE
51g PROTEIN	15g FAT	1.5g FIBER

1½ lb	(750 g) ground beef
1	egg
2 tbsp	(30 ml) breadcrumbs
1 tbsp	(15 ml) chopped parsley
½ tsp	(2 ml) Worcestershire sauce
2 tbsp	(30 ml) vegetable oil
1	onion, chopped
1 lb	(500 g) mushrooms, sliced
2 tbsp	(30 ml) green peppercorns
1½ cups	(375 ml) beef stock, heated
1 tbsp	(15 ml) cornstarch
3 tbsp	(45 ml) cold water
	salt

Mix meat, egg, breadcrumbs, parsley and Worcestershire sauce in mixer for 2 minutes at high speed; season to taste. Shape into steaks.

Heat oil in large frying pan. Cook steaks 8 to 10 minutes over medium heat turning over 4 times. When cooked, remove and keep hot in oven.

Add onion to frying pan and cook 2 minutes. Add mushrooms and peppercorns, season and continue cooking 3 to 4 minutes over medium heat.

Pour in beef stock, mix and bring to boil. Mix cornstarch with water and stir into sauce. Cook 2 minutes more to thicken.

Remove steaks from oven and serve with sauce.

Salisbury Steak

(serves 4)

1 SERVING	436 CALORIES	16g CARBOHYDRATE
57g PROTEIN	16g FAT	2.1g FIBER

2 lb	(900 g) ground beef
2 tbsp	(30 ml) breadcrumbs
1	egg
1 tbsp	(15 ml) chopped parsley
½ tsp	(2 ml) chili powder
2 tbsp	(30 ml) vegetable oil
4	onions, thinly sliced
2 tbsp	(30 ml) tomato paste
½ tsp	(2 ml) basil
2 cups	(500 ml) beef stock, heated
1½ tbsp	(25 ml) cornstarch
3 tbsp	(45 ml) cold water
	salt and pepper

Preheat oven to 150°F (70°C).

Mix meat, breadcrumbs, egg, parsley, chili powder, salt and pepper together until well incorporated. Shape into steaks.

Heat oil in large frying pan. Cook 8 to 10 minutes over medium heat. Turn over 4 times and season twice. When cooked, remove from pan and keep hot in oven.

Add onions to pan; cook 4 minutes over medium heat.

Add tomato paste and mix well. Stir in basil and beef stock; bring to boil. Correct seasoning.

Mix cornstarch with water; stir into sauce and cook 3 to 4 minutes.

Pour onion sauce over steaks and serve.

Braised Beef Brisket

(serves 4)

1 SERVING	558 CALORIES	5g CARBOHYDRATE
22g PROTEIN	50g FAT	0.5g FIBER

2 tbsp	(30 ml) vegetable oil
4 lb	(1.8 kg) beef brisket, tied
2	large onions, thinly sliced
1	clove
2 tbsp	(30 ml) paprika
¼ tsp	(1 ml) thyme
1 tsp	(5 ml) chopped parsley
1 cup	(250 ml) beer
2 cups	(500 ml) light beef stock, heated
2 tbsp	(30 ml) cornstarch
4 tbsp	(60 ml) cold water
¼ cup	(50 ml) sour cream
	salt and pepper

Preheat oven to 350°F (180°C).

Heat oil in ovenproof casserole. Sear beef 8 minutes on all sides over medium heat. Remove and season well.

Add onions to casserole and cook 4 minutes.

Stir in seasonings and parsley; cook 2 minutes.

Pour in beer, bring to boil and cook 3 minutes over medium heat. Replace meat in casserole and add beef stock; correct seasoning and bring to boil again.

Cover casserole and finish cooking 2-2½ hours in oven. Meat should be very tender when served.

When done, remove meat from casserole and set aside.

Place casserole over medium heat and bring liquid to boil. Mix cornstarch with water; stir into sauce and continue cooking 3 minutes.

Remove from heat, stir in sour cream and serve sauce with meat.

Italian Sausages and Vegetables

(serves 4)

1 SERVING	276 CALORIES	31g CARBOHYDRATE
11g PROTEIN	12g FAT	3.6g FIBER

2	carrots, pared and sliced on the bias 1 in (2.5 cm) thick
24	fresh pearl onions
1	small zucchini, sliced on the bias 1 in (2.5 cm) thick
2 tbsp	(30 ml) vegetable oil
2	apples, peeled, cored and in wedges
4	Italian sausages, sliced on the bias 1 in (2.5 cm) thick
2	garlic cloves, smashed and chopped
1½ cups	(375 ml) chicken stock, heated
1 tbsp	(15 ml) tomato paste
1 tbsp	(15 ml) cornstarch
3 tbsp	(45 ml) cold water
	salt and pepper

Place carrots in saucepan, cover with water and boil 6 minutes uncovered.

Add onions and zucchini; season and cook 3 minutes. Drain vegetables and let cool slightly.

Heat oil in large frying pan. Cook vegetables, apples, sausages and garlic 4 to 5 minutes over high heat; season well.

Pour in chicken stock and bring to boil.

Stir in tomato paste and cook 1 minute over medium-low heat. Mix cornstarch with water; stir into sauce and finish cooking 1 minute.

Serve with rice.

Creamy Chicken Stew

(serves 4)

1 SERVING	333 CALORIES	29g CARBOHYDRATE
25g PROTEIN	13g FAT	2.7g FIBER

3½ lb	(1.6 kg) chicken, cut in 10 pieces and skinned
1	small onion, coarsely chopped
1	celery stalk, diced
1	bay leaf
1	parsley sprig
¼ tsp	(1 ml) celery salt
½ tsp	(2 ml) basil
3 tbsp	(45 ml) butter
4 tbsp	(60 ml) flour
2	large cooked carrots, diced large
1	large cooked potato, diced large
1	cooked parsnip, diced large
	salt and pepper
	paprika

Season chicken pieces with salt, pepper and paprika. Place leg and thigh pieces in large skillet and cover with cold water.

Add onion, celery, bay leaf, parsley and seasonings. Cover and bring to boil. Continue cooking 16 minutes over medium heat.

Add remaining chicken pieces and continue cooking 20 minutes covered.

Transfer chicken pieces to bowl and strain cooking liquid through fine sieve into second bowl.

Heat butter in skillet. Mix in flour and cook 2 to 3 minutes over low heat, stirring occasionally.

Pour in half of strained cooking liquid and whisk well. Incorporate remaining and season. Cook sauce 3 to 4 minutes over medium heat.

Place cooked vegetables in sauce and cook 3 to 4 minutes over medium-low heat.

Add chicken and finish cooking 8 to 10 minutes over low heat. Do not cover.

Cut chicken in 10 pieces and skin. Season with salt, pepper and paprika.

Cover with cold water. Add onion, celery, bay leaf, parsley and seasonings. Cover pan and bring to boil.

Place leg and thigh pieces in large skillet.

After all chicken has been cooked and removed, add vegetables to sauce.

Roast Chicken

(serves 4)

1 SERVING	321 CALORIES	12g CARBOHYDRATE
30g PROTEIN	17g FAT	1.9g FIBER

4-5 lb	(1.8 - 2.3 kg) chicken, cleaned
1	large carrot
2	celery stalks
1	onion, cut in half
2-3	parsley sprigs
1	bay leaf
3 tbsp	(45 ml) melted butter
1	onion, diced
½ tsp	(2 ml) tarragon
1½ cups	(375 ml) hot chicken stock
1½ tbsp	(25 ml) cornstarch
3 tbsp	(45 ml) cold water
	salt and pepper

Preheat oven to 425°F (220°C).

Stuff cleaned chicken with carrot, celery, halved onion, parsley and bay leaf. Force inside and dribble in 1 tsp (5 ml) melted butter.

Secure legs with string and baste with remaining butter. Place in roasting pan, season generously and sear about 15 minutes in oven.

Reduce heat to 350°F (180°C) and finish cooking chicken 25 to 30 minutes per 1 lb (500 g).

When cooked, remove chicken and set aside.

Place roasting pan over high heat; add diced onion and tarragon and cook 4 minutes.

Pour in chicken stock and bring to boil. Season and continue cooking 3 to 4 minutes.

Mix cornstarch with water; stir into sauce and cook 1 to 2 minutes or until thickened.

Serve onion gravy with chicken.

1 Stuff cleaned chicken with vegetables, parsley and bay leaf. Force inside and dribble in 1 tsp (5 ml) melted butter.

3 Place in roasting pan, season generously and baste with remaining butter. Sear about 15 minutes in oven.

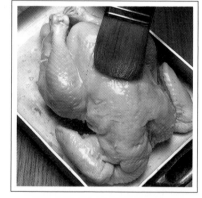

2 Secure chicken by drawing a string threaded on a trussing needle through the legs twice. Knot string between legs.

4 After chicken is cooked, prepare gravy by using juices that have collected in roasting pan.

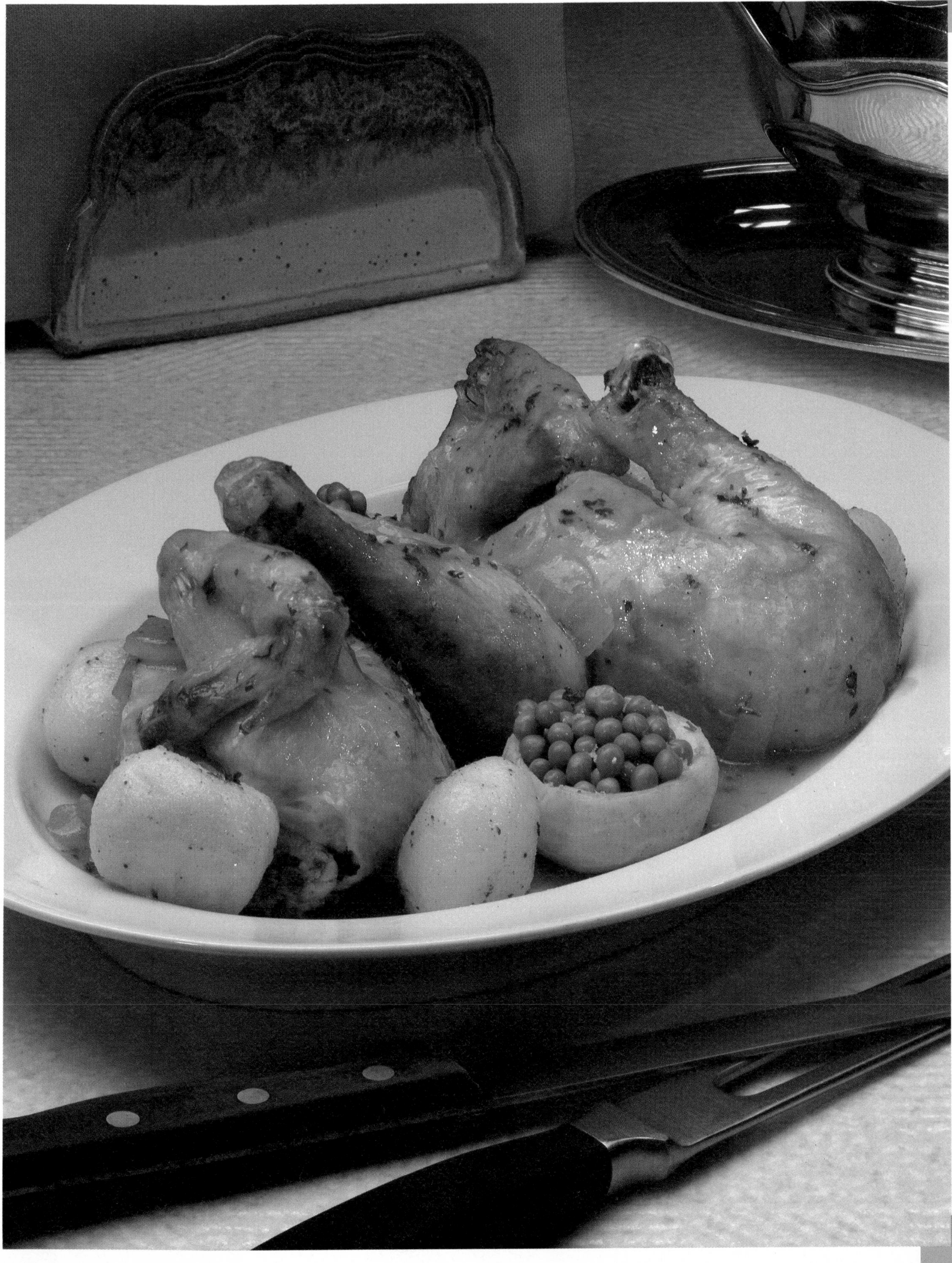

Pineapple Chicken

(serves 4)

1 SERVING	252 CALORIES	14g CARBOHYDRATE
22g PROTEIN	12g FAT	0.5g FIBER

2 tbsp	(30 ml) vegetable oil
2	chicken breasts, skinned, halved and cubed
1 tbsp	(15 ml) chopped ginger
3 tbsp	(45 ml) pine nuts
14 oz	(398 ml) can pineapple chunks
3 tbsp	(45 ml) wine vinegar
1½ cups	(375 ml) chicken stock, heated
1 tsp	(5 ml) soya sauce
1 tbsp	(15 ml) cornstarch
3 tbsp	(45 ml) cold water
	salt and pepper

Heat oil in large frying pan. Add chicken, ginger and pine nuts; season and cook 4 to 5 minutes. Stir once.

Drain pineapple and reserve ½ cup (125 ml) of juice. Add pineapple chunks to pan and continue cooking 3 to 4 minutes over low heat.

Remove chicken pieces and set aside.

Add vinegar to sauce and boil 1 minute. Stir in pineapple juice, chicken stock and soya sauce; season well and bring to boil. Cook 3 minutes.

Mix cornstarch with water; stir into sauce and bring to boil. Cook 1 more minute.

Replace chicken in pan, correct seasoning and simmer over low heat until heated through.

Chicken Livers Marsala

(serves 4)

1 SERVING	397 CALORIES	21g CARBOHYDRATE
40g PROTEIN	17g FAT	0.8g FIBER

1½ lb	(750 g) chicken livers, cleaned, fat trimmed and halved
½ cup	(125 ml) seasoned flour
2 tbsp	(30 ml) vegetable oil
1 tbsp	(15 ml) butter
1	small onion, finely chopped
½ lb	(250 g) mushrooms, sliced
1 tbsp	(15 ml) chopped parsley
½ cup	(125 ml) Marsala wine
1 cup	(250 ml) chicken stock, heated
1 tsp	(5 ml) cornstarch
2 tbsp	(30 ml) cold water
	salt and pepper

Dredge livers in flour. Heat oil and butter in large frying pan. Cook livers 4 minutes over high heat, stirring once.

Add onion, mushrooms and parsley; season and continue cooking 4 to 5 minutes over medium heat.

Pour in wine and chicken stock; mix and cook 4 minutes over low heat.

Mix cornstarch with water; stir into sauce and bring to boil. Simmer 2 minutes over low heat and serve with noodles.

Pork Tenderloin Sauté

(serves 4)

1 SERVING	357 CALORIES	12g CARBOHYDRATE
30g PROTEIN	21g FAT	1.5g FIBER

2	pork tenderloins
2 tbsp	(30 ml) soya sauce
¼ cup	(50 ml) dry sherry
3 tbsp	(45 ml) vegetable oil
1	leek, (white part only) thinly sliced
½ lb	(250 g) mushrooms, sliced
3	green onions, in sticks
1	green pepper, thinly sliced
½ cup	(125 ml) frozen peas, cooked
2 cups	(500 ml) chicken stock, heated
2 tbsp	(30 ml) cornstarch
4 tbsp	(60 ml) cold water
	salt and pepper

Trim meat of fat and slice on the bias ¾ in (2 cm) thick. Place in bowl with soya sauce and sherry; marinate 30 minutes.

Remove meat from bowl; reserve marinade.

Heat 1½ tbsp (25 ml) oil in frying pan. Cook half of meat for 3 to 4 minutes over medium heat; turn pieces over once and season well.

Remove cooked meat, set aside and repeat for remaining meat but avoid adding any more oil.

When all meat is cooked and removed, add rest of oil to pan. Cook vegetables 3 to 4 minutes over high heat; season well.

Pour in chicken stock and reserved marinade; bring to boil.

Mix cornstarch with water; stir into sauce and cook 1 to 2 minutes over medium heat.

Replace meat in sauce, simmer 3 to 4 minutes and serve.

1 For convenience gather all the ingredients needed before you start the recipe.

2 Place all meat, parsley and seasonings in large bowl. Add onion and garlic; mix well.

Mushroom Sauce for Meatloaf

1 SERVING 30 CALORIES 2g CARBOHYDRATE
1g PROTEIN 2g FAT 0.2g FIBER

2 tbsp	(30 ml) vegetable oil
½ lb	(250 g) mushrooms, sliced
2 tbsp	(30 ml) chopped onion
1 cup	(250 ml) peeled diced eggplant
2 cups	(500 ml) beef stock, heated
1 tbsp	(15 ml) chopped chives
2 tbsp	(30 ml) cornstarch
4 tbsp	(60 ml) cold water
	salt and pepper

Heat oil in frying pan. Add mushrooms, onion and eggplant; cover and cook 10 minutes over low heat. Season well.

Add beef stock, chives and season well; bring to boil.

Mix cornstarch with water; stir into sauce and cook 4 to 5 minutes over low heat.

Pour sauce over meatloaf or serve with burgers.

The Best Meatloaf

(serves 6 to 8)

1 SERVING 317 CALORIES 14g CARBOHYDRATE
36g PROTEIN 13g FAT 0.3g FIBER

1 lb	(500 g) ground beef
½ lb	(250 g) ground pork
½ lb	(250 g) ground veal
1 tbsp	(15 ml) chopped parsley
¼ tsp	(1 ml) thyme
¼ tsp	(1 ml) chili powder
¼ tsp	(1 ml) basil
1	onion, chopped and cooked
2	garlic cloves, smashed and chopped
1½ cups	(375 ml) breadcrumbs
2	eggs
1 cup	(250 ml) light cream
	salt and pepper
	several bay leaves

Preheat oven to 350°F (180°C).

Set aside 10 × 4 in (25 × 10 cm) mold.

Place all meat, parsley and seasonings in large bowl. Add onion and garlic; mix well.

Add breadcrumbs and eggs; mix, then stir in cream.

To double-check seasoning, cook a tiny patty of mixture in hot oil. Taste and adjust remaining mixture if necessary.

Press mixture into loaf pan, place bay leaves on top and set in roasting pan with hot water. Cook 1½ hours in oven.

Serve plain or with mushroom sauce.

3 Add breadcrumbs and eggs, mix then stir in cream.

4 Press mixture into loaf pan, place bay leaves on top and set in roasting pan with hot water.

Meatballs and Garlic Spinach

(serves 4)

1 SERVING	446 CALORIES	14g CARBOHYDRATE
57g PROTEIN	18g FAT	1.9g FIBER

1½ lb	(750 g) lean ground pork
1	onion, chopped and cooked
¼ tsp	(1 ml) chili powder
1 tsp	(5 ml) Worcestershire sauce
1	egg
2 tbsp	(30 ml) vegetable oil
1½ cups	(375 ml) chicken stock, heated
1 tbsp	(15 ml) soya sauce
1 tbsp	(15 ml) cornstarch
3 tbsp	(45 ml) cold water
2	garlic cloves, smashed and chopped
2 lb	(900 g) spinach, cooked and chopped
	salt and pepper

In mixer blend together pork, onion, chili powder, Worcestershire sauce, egg, salt and pepper. When mixture is smooth, shape into small meatballs.

Heat half of oil in large frying pan. Add meatballs and cook 3 to 4 minutes on all sides; season generously.

Using small spoon remove most of fat from pan and discard. Add chicken stock and soya sauce to meatballs. Cover and cook 6 minutes over low heat.

Mix cornstarch with water; stir into meatball mixture and continue cooking 3 minutes.

Meanwhile, heat remaining oil in second frying pan. When hot, cook garlic and spinach 3 minutes over medium heat; season well.

Serve spinach with meatballs.

Pork Shoulder Roast with Cider

(serves 4)

1 SERVING	1107 CALORIES	32g CARBOHYDRATE
112g PROTEIN	59g FAT	2.2g FIBER

2 tbsp	(30 ml) vegetable oil
5 lb	(2.3 kg) pork shoulder, fat trimmed and tied
2	onions, thinly sliced
2	apples, peeled, cored and in wedges
2 cups	(500 ml) apple cider
1 cup	(250 ml) chicken stock, heated
¼ tsp	(1 ml) thyme
½ tsp	(2 ml) basil
½ cup	(125 ml) sultana raisins
1 tbsp	(15 ml) cornstarch
2 tbsp	(30 ml) cold water
	salt and pepper

Preheat oven to 300°F (150°C).

Heat oil in ovenproof casserole. Sear meat 8 minutes on all sides over medium heat. Remove and season well; set aside.

Add onions and apple to casserole; cook 5 to 6 minutes.

Add cider and bring to boil; cook 2 minutes.

Add chicken stock, mix well and replace meat in sauce. Add seasonings and bring to boil with cover.

Finish cooking meat 2 to 2½ hours in oven with cover.

When done, transfer meat to serving platter. Place casserole over medium heat; bring liquid to boil and skim.

Stir in raisins. Mix cornstarch with water; stir into sauce and cook 1 minute. Correct seasoning.

Serve sauce with pork.

Rice Hash Pancakes

(serves 4)

| 1 SERVING | 396 CALORIES | 28g CARBOHYDRATE |
| 17g PROTEIN | 24g FAT | 1.0g FIBER |

3 tbsp	(45 ml) oil
1	onion, finely chopped
¾ cup	(175 ml) ground beef
1 tbsp	(15 ml) chopped parsley
¼ tsp	(1 ml) ground clove
2 tbsp	(30 ml) flour
1½ cups	(375 ml) leftover cooked rice
½ cup	(125 ml) grated Gruyère cheese
1	egg
2 tbsp	(30 ml) butter
2 cups	(500 ml) spicy tomato sauce, heated
	salt and pepper
	Parmesan cheese to taste

Heat oil in frying pan. Cook onion 3 minutes over low heat.

Add beef, season. Add parsley and clove; mix and cook 3 to 4 minutes over medium heat.

Mix in flour and rice. Add Gruyère cheese and mix again; cook 3 minutes.

Cool, then add egg. Transfer to mixer; blend 2 minutes.

Dust hands with flour and shape mixture into pancakes. Cook 4 minutes each side in hot butter.

Serve with tomato sauce and Parmesan cheese.

Tomato Rice

(serves 4)

1 SERVING	209 CALORIES	35g CARBOHYDRATE
6g PROTEIN	5g FAT	1.5g FIBER

1 tbsp	(15 ml) olive oil
1	onion, chopped
1	garlic clove, smashed and chopped
1 tbsp	(15 ml) chopped parsley
1½ cups	(375 ml) canned tomatoes, drained and chopped
1 cup	(250 ml) long grain rice, rinsed
1 tbsp	(15 ml) tomato paste
1¼ cups	(300 ml) tomato juice
½ cup	(125 ml) grated Parmesan cheese
	salt and pepper

Preheat oven to 350°F (180°C).

Heat oil in ovenproof casserole. Cook onion, garlic and parsley 2 minutes over medium heat.

Stir in tomatoes and cook 3 minutes over high heat; season.

Mix in rice, tomato paste and juice; bring to boil.

Cover and cook 18 minutes in oven.

About 5 minutes before rice is cooked, stir in cheese with fork.

Vegetable Baked Rice

(serves 4)

1 SERVING	242 CALORIES	33g CARBOHYDRATE
5g PROTEIN	10g FAT	3.7g FIBER

1 tbsp	(15 ml) olive oil
3	green onions, finely chopped
1 cup	(250 ml) long grain rice, rinsed
¼ tsp	(1 ml) thyme
1	bay leaf
1½ cups	(375 ml) chicken stock, heated
2 tbsp	(30 ml) butter
¼	celery stalk, diced
½ cup	(125 ml) cooked green peas
½ cup	(125 ml) cooked diced carrots
½ cup	(125 ml) diced zucchini
½ cup	(125 ml) diced mushrooms
	salt and pepper

Preheat oven to 350°F (180°C).

Heat oil in ovenproof casserole and cook onions 3 minutes over low heat.

Stir in rice; cook 2 minutes over medium heat. Season and mix in thyme and bay leaf.

Pour in chicken stock; cover and bring to boil. Finish cooking 18 minutes in oven.

Meanwhile, heat butter in frying pan. When hot, add all vegetables and cook about 3 to 4 minutes. Season generously. Add these vegetables to casserole about 5 minutes before rice is done.

Celeriac Pancakes

(serves 4)

1 SERVING	409 CALORIES	37g CARBOHYDRATE
18g PROTEIN	21g FAT	1.6g FIBER

1 lb	(500 g) celeriac, peeled and in lemony water
4	large potatoes, peeled and blanched 15 minutes
1½ cups	(375 ml) grated Gruyère cheese
2 tbsp	(30 ml) vegetable oil
	salt and pepper

Preheat oven to 425°F (220°C).

Dry celeriac and cut into very fine julienne; place in bowl. Cut potatoes in fine julienne and add to bowl along with cheese; season everything well and mix. Chill 1 hour.

Heat oil in large frying pan. When hot, place celeriac mixture in pan and press down with spatula. Cook 15 minutes over medium heat.

Wrap frying pan handle in foil and finish cooking pancake in oven for 15 minutes.

Slice as you would a pizza and serve.

Potato Pancakes

(serves 4)

1 SERVING	408 CALORIES	34g CARBOHYDRATE
5g PROTEIN	28g FAT	2.0g FIBER

8	potatoes, peeled and boiled
3 tbsp	(45 ml) butter
2	egg yolks
½ tsp	(2 ml) ginger
½ tsp	(2 ml) savory
1 tsp	(5 ml) sesame seeds
¼ cup	(50 ml) heavy cream
3 tbsp	(45 ml) peanut oil
	salt and white pepper

Mash potatoes through food mill. Add remaining ingredients (except oil) and mix until thoroughly blended. Set aside to cool.

Dust hands with flour and shape mixture into small pancakes. Heat oil in large frying pan and cook 3 minutes each side over medium-high heat.

Serve immediately.

Shepherd's Pie

(serves 4 to 6)

1 SERVING	587 CALORIES	44g CARBOHYDRATE
42g PROTEIN	27g FAT	3.9g FIBER

2 tbsp	(30 ml) oil
½	red onion, chopped
1 tbsp	(15 ml) chopped parsley
½ lb	(250 g) mushrooms, coarsely chopped
¼ tsp	(1 ml) ground clove
¼ tsp	(1 ml) allspice
1 lb	(500 g) ground beef
½ lb	(250 g) ground pork
½ tsp	(2 ml) basil

¼ tsp	(1 ml) thyme
12 oz	(341 ml) can whole kernel corn, drained
1½ cups	(375 ml) hot tomato sauce
½ cup	(125 ml) grated Romano cheese
3-3½ cups	(750-875 ml)) mashed potatoes
2 tbsp	(30 ml) melted butter
	salt and pepper
	dash paprika

Preheat oven to 375°F (190°C).

Heat oil in skillet and cook onion and parsley 2 minutes. Add mushrooms, clove and allspice; continue cooking 3 minutes over medium heat.

Stir in beef and pork, add basil and thyme; cook 5 to 6 minutes over medium-high heat.

Mix in corn, season and cook 3 to 4 minutes. Add tomato sauce, cheese and continue cooking 2 to 3 minutes over medium heat.

Spoon mixture into large baking dish and completely cover with mashed potatoes. Use a pastry bag for a fancy top as shown in the picture.

Sprinkle potatoes with paprika and moisten slightly with melted butter. Bake 45 minutes in oven.

Cook mushrooms, clove and allspice 3 minutes over medium heat.

Mix in corn, season and cook 3 to 4 minutes. Then add tomato sauce, cheese and continue cooking 2 to 3 minutes.

Add beef, pork, basil and thyme; cook 5 to 6 minutes over medium-high heat.

Spoon mixture into large baking dish and cover with mashed potatoes. If you desire a fancy top, use a pastry bag.

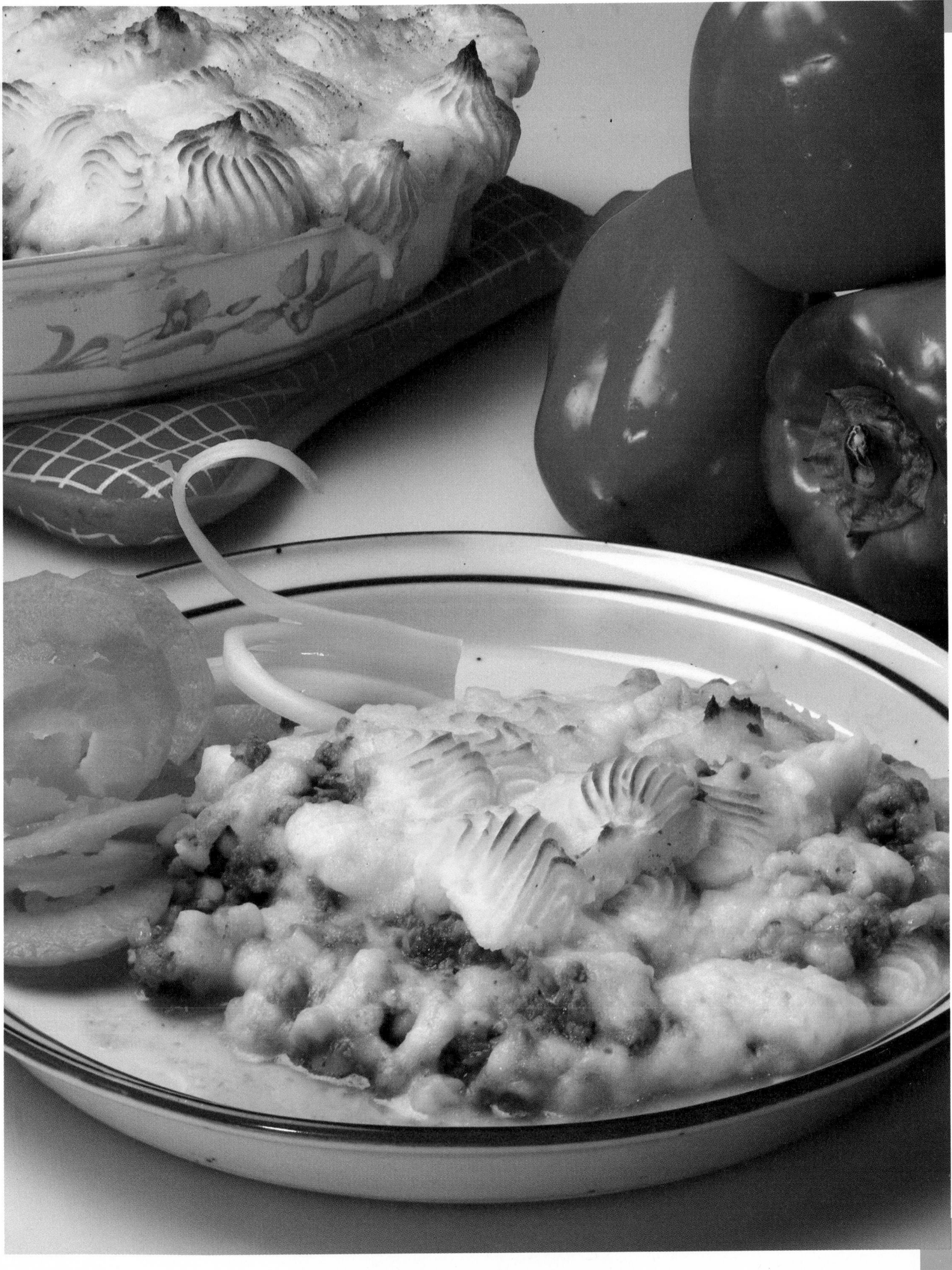

Pita Pizza

(serves 4)

1 SERVING	553 CALORIES	57g CARBOHYDRATE
25g PROTEIN	25g FAT	3.9g FIBER

4	small whole wheat pita bread
1 - 1½ cups	tomato sauce, heated
12	mushrooms, sliced
½	green pepper, in rings
½	red pepper, in rings
12	pitted black olives, sliced
2	raw sausages
1 cup	(250 ml) grated mozzarella cheese
1¼ cups	(300 ml) grated cheddar cheese
	chopped parsley to taste
	salt and pepper

Preheat oven to 425°F (220°C).

Place pita bread on cookie sheet and cover with tomato sauce. Add mushrooms, peppers and olives.

Remove sausage meat from casing and arrange on pizzas in tiny clumps. Top with a mixture of grated cheeses and season with parsley, salt and pepper.

Cook pizzas in the middle of the oven for 10 minutes.

Pita pizzas are a great way to use leftover vegetables — be creative with what's in your fridge.

Hot Potato Salad

(serves 4)

1 SERVING	180 CALORIES	27g CARBOHYDRATE
9g PROTEIN	4g FAT	1.4g FIBER

4	large potatoes, boiled with skin and still hot
4	slices bacon, diced
3	green onions, chopped
1	stalk celery heart, finely chopped
1	garlic clove, smashed and chopped
½ cup	(125 ml) red wine vinegar
¾ cup	(175 ml) chicken stock, heated
1 tbsp	(15 ml) chopped chives
	salt and pepper

Peel and cut potatoes in thick slices. Place in oven at 150°F (70°C) to keep hot.

Cook bacon in frying pan for 4 minutes or until crisp. Remove bacon leaving fat in pan and set aside.

Add onions, celery and garlic to pan; cook 3 minutes over medium heat.

Mix in vinegar; cook 1 minute over high heat. Add chicken stock and continue cooking 2 minutes.

Stir in chives and season generously. Pour over hot potatoes and let stand 10 minutes on counter.

Serve on lettuce leaves and sprinkle portions with reserved bacon.

Sole Croquettes

(serves 4)

1 SERVING	543 CALORIES	42g CARBOHYDRATE
33g PROTEIN	27g FAT	0.2g FIBER

4 tbsp	(60 ml) butter
3½ tbsp	(50 ml) flour
1 cup	(250 ml) hot milk
3	sole filets, cooked and chopped
1	small envelope unflavored gelatine, softened in water
1	egg yolk
¼ cup	(50 ml) heavy cream
1 tbsp	(15 ml) chopped parsley
3	egg whites
1 tbsp	(15 ml) oil
2 cups	(500 ml) breadcrumbs
	salt and pepper
	juice ¼ lemon

Heat butter in saucepan. Add flour and mix; cook 2 minutes over low heat.

Whisk in milk and season; continue cooking 5 minutes.

Remove saucepan from heat. Stir in fish and gelatine. Mix egg yolk with cream and incorporate.

Stir in parsley, lemon juice and correct seasoning. Spread mixture on large dinner plate, cover with plastic wrap and chill 2 minutes.

Beat egg whites with oil just until slightly foamy.

Shape croquette mixture into tubes; roll in breadcrumbs then dip in egg whites and finish by rolling in breadcrumbs again.

Deep-fry sole croquettes in hot oil until evenly browned.

Cheese Stuffed Tomatoes

(serves 4)

1 SERVING	180 CALORIES	18g CARBOHYDRATE
9g PROTEIN	8g FAT	3.2g FIBER

4	large tomatoes
1 tbsp	(15 ml) vegetable oil
1	small onion, finely chopped
1	garlic clove, smashed and chopped
½ tsp	(2 ml) oregano
15	mushrooms, sliced
1 tbsp	(15 ml) chopped parsley
½ cup	(125 ml) ricotta cheese
⅓ cup	(75 ml) breadcrumbs
	salt and pepper

Preheat oven to 375°F (190°C).

Core tomatoes, turn them upside-down and cut away a top. Scoop out most of flesh but leave a sturdy shell. Place shells in baking dish, season insides and moisten with a sprinkle of oil. Set tomato flesh aside.

Heat oil in frying pan and cook onion and garlic 3 to 4 minutes.

Add tomato flesh, oregano, mushrooms and parsley. Season well and cook 4 to 5 minutes over medium heat.

Mix in cheese and breadcrumbs; cook 2 to 3 minutes over medium heat.

Fill tomato shells with mixture and bake 30 to 35 minutes in oven.

Core tomatoes, turn them upside-down and cut away a top. You can keep the tops for decoration at serving time.

After onion and garlic have cooked, add tomato flesh, oregano, mushrooms and parsley. Season well and cook 4 to 5 minutes over medium heat.

Scoop out most of flesh but leave a sturdy shell. Season insides and set shells aside.

Mix in cheese and breadcrumbs; cook 2 to 3 minutes then fill tomato shells with mixture. Bake 30 to 35 minutes in oven.

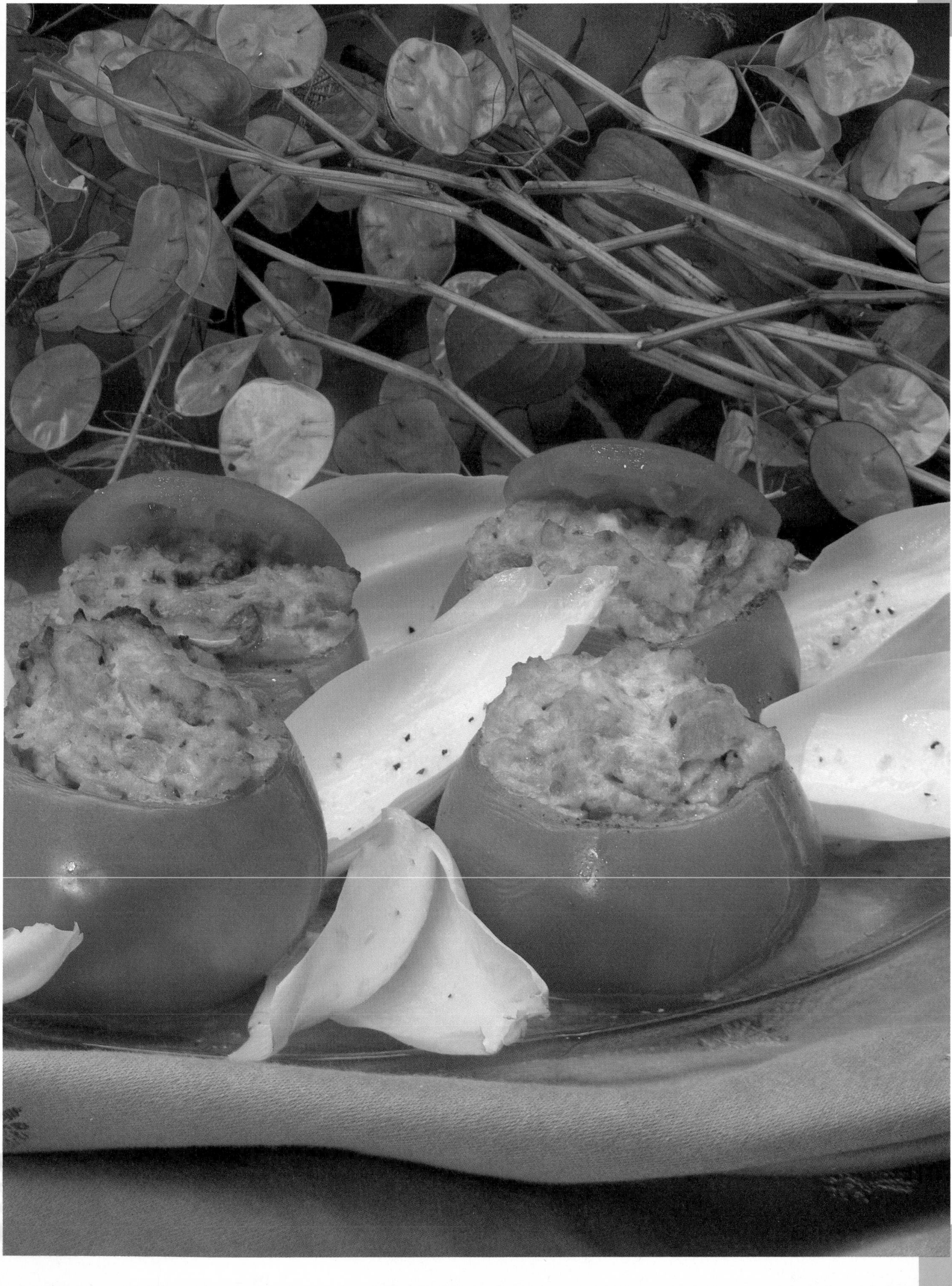

Potato Salad with Lemon Dressing

(serves 4)

1 SERVING	291 CALORIES	18g CARBOHYDRATE
3g PROTEIN	23g FAT	1.4g FIBER

½ cup	(125 ml) mayonnaise
1 tbsp	(15 ml) chopped parsley
2 tbsp	(30 ml) grated lemon rind
4	boiled potatoes, peeled and diced large
2	celery stalks, diced
¼ cup	(50 ml) chopped red onion
	juice ½ lemon
	salt and pepper

Mix mayonnaise, parsley, lemon rind and juice together; season to taste.

Place potatoes, celery and onion in bowl; toss together.

Pour in lemon dressing, toss again and serve.

Beef Tongue Salad

(serves 4)

1 SERVING	232 CALORIES	10g CARBOHYDRATE
12g PROTEIN	16g FAT	

1	large cucumber, peeled, seeded and in julienne
1	apple, peeled, cored and in wedges
1 cup	(250 ml) cooked beets, in julienne
2 cups	(500 ml) cooked beef tongue, in julienne
3 tbsp	(45 ml) capers
¼ cup	(50 ml) mayonnaise
1 tbsp	(15 ml) strong mustard
1 tbsp	(15 ml) anchovy paste
	few drops lemon juice
	salt and pepper

Place cucumber in bowl, sprinkle with salt and marinate 30 minutes on counter.

Drain liquid and transfer cucumber to clean bowl. Add apple, beets, tongue and capers; mix.

Stir mayonnaise, mustard, anchovy paste, lemon juice and salt and pepper together. Pour over salad ingredients and mix until well coated.

Serve on lettuce leaves.

Delicious Turkey Salad

(serves 4)

1 SERVING	262 CALORIES	11g CARBOHYDRATE
23g PROTEIN	14g FAT	2.3g FIBER

2 cups	(500 ml) leftover cooked turkey, diced
2	carrots, pared and grated
½ cup	(125 ml) finely chopped onion
2	green onions, finely chopped
1	celery stalk, diced
1	cucumber, peeled, seeded and sliced
24	mushrooms, sliced
¼ cup	(50 ml) lime juice
2	mint leaves, chopped
3 oz	(90 g) cream cheese, soft
1 tbsp	(15 ml) oil
1 tsp	(5 ml) wine vinegar
	few drops Worcestershire sauce
	salt and pepper

Place all vegetables in large salad bowl.

In blender, mix together remaining ingredients until smooth. Pour dressing over salad, chill and serve.

Leftover Vegetable Soup

(serves 6 to 8)

1 SERVING	140 CALORIES	22g CARBOHYDRATE
4g PROTEIN	4g FAT	2.4g FIBER

2 tbsp	(30 ml) melted butter
2	onions, chopped
2	green onions, sliced
2	carrots, pared and sliced
2	potatoes, peeled and diced
1	small turnip, peeled and sliced
1	parsnip, pared and sliced
1	bay leaf
3	parsley sprigs
½ tsp	(2 ml) basil
¼ tsp	(1 ml) rosemary
½ tsp	(2 ml) chervil
¼ tsp	(1 ml) marjoram
¼	cabbage, in leaves
8 cups	(2 L) chicken stock, heated
1	yellow pepper, diced
1	red pepper, diced
1½ cups	(375 ml) large croutons
¼ cup	(50 ml) grated Gruyère cheese
	salt and pepper

Heat butter in very large saucepan. Add both onions and cook 3 minutes covered over medium heat.

Add carrots, potatoes, turnip and parsnip; mix well. Cover and continue cooking 5 minutes.

Add all seasonings including bay leaf and parsley; mix well and stir in cabbage. Pour in chicken stock and bring to boil uncovered over high heat.

Cook soup 35 minutes uncovered over medium-low heat.

About 5 minutes before soup is done, add peppers. Serve with croutons and garnish portions with grated cheese.

Scrambled Eggs with Vegetables

(serves 4)

1 SERVING	251 CALORIES	5g CARBOHYDRATE
15g PROTEIN	19g FAT	1.3g FIBER

2 tbsp	(30 ml) butter
12	cherry tomatoes
¼	cucumber, diced small
4	green onions, in 1 in (2.5 cm) sticks
8	beaten eggs, seasoned
6	slices salami, in strips
	salt and pepper

Heat butter in nonstick pan. When hot, add vegetables and cook 3 to 4 minutes over medium-high heat. Season well and stir once.

Reduce heat to medium and pour in eggs. Mix rapidly and continue cooking 1 to 2 minutes while stirring.

Add salami strips, mix and serve immediately. Accompany with bacon if desired.

Flat Spinach and Cheese Omelet

(serves 2)

1 SERVING	441 CALORIES	5g CARBOHYDRATE
31g PROTEIN	33g FAT	0.8g FIBER

2 tbsp	(30 ml) butter
1½ cups	(375 ml) cooked chopped spinach
6	eggs
½ cup	(125 ml) grated Gruyère cheese
	salt and pepper

Heat 1 tbsp (15 ml) butter in nonstick frying pan. When hot, add spinach and season well. Cook 3 minutes over high heat.

Break eggs into bowl and beat with fork; season well.

Remove spinach from pan and pour into eggs; mix well.

Heat remaining butter in nonstick pan. When hot, pour in egg mixture and cook 3 minutes over medium heat.

Sprinkle top with cheese; cover and cook 2 to 3 minutes over medium-low heat.

Slide omelet out of pan and serve.

Potato Omelet

(serves 2)

1 SERVING	441 CALORIES	18g CARBOHYDRATE
18g PROTEIN	33g FAT	1.1g FIBER

2 tbsp	(30 ml) butter
1 tsp	(5 ml) vegetable oil
2	potatoes, peeled and sliced
2 tbsp	(30 ml) chopped onion
1 tbsp	(15 ml) chopped fresh parsley
5	eggs
	pinch nutmeg
	salt and pepper

Heat 1 tbsp (15 ml) butter and oil in small frying pan.

When hot, add potatoes and season well. Cook 2 to 3 minutes on each side over medium heat. Stir once during cooking process.

Sprinkle nutmeg over potatoes and mix; cover and continue cooking 8 to 10 minutes.

Mix well; add onion and parsley. Cook, uncovered, 3 to 4 minutes. Meanwhile, break eggs into bowl and beat with fork; season well.

Heat remaining butter in nonstick frying pan or omelet pan.

When hot, pour in eggs and cook 1 minute over high heat.

Stir eggs rapidly and add potatoes. Roll omelet (see technique) and continue cooking 1 minute.

Serve with cooked broccoli and decorate with several cooked potatoes.

Stuffed Egg Halves with Mustard

(serves 4 to 6)

1 SERVING	241 CALORIES	0g CARBOHYDRATE
13g PROTEIN	21g FAT	0.2g FIBER

12	hard-boiled eggs, cut in half lengthwise
2 tbsp	(30 ml) Dijon mustard
4 tbsp	(60 ml) mayonnaise
	several drops Tabasco sauce
	lemon juice to taste
	salt and white pepper
	chopped fresh parsley
	several lettuce leaves, washed and dried

Force egg yolks through sieve using back of wooden spoon. Place in mixing bowl.

Add mustard, mayonnaise, Tabasco sauce, lemon juice, salt and pepper. Mix until well combined and correct seasoning.

Spoon mixture into pastry bag fitted with star nozzle. Stuff egg whites; sprinkle with some parsley.

Place stuffed eggs on lettuce leaves and serve.

If desired, refrigerate until serving time. Cover with plastic wrap.

Poached Eggs with Bacon

(serves 2)

1 SERVING	288 CALORIES	1g CARBOHYDRATE
17g PROTEIN	24g FAT	0g FIBER

6 cups	(1.5 L) water
1 tsp	(5 ml) white vinegar
4	eggs
6	slices bacon, cooked crisp
	salt
	buttered toast

Place water, vinegar and salt in large saucepan; bring to boil.

Reduce heat so that water simmers. Carefully slide eggs, one at a time, into water. Cook 3 minutes over medium heat.

Remove eggs with slotted spoon and drain.

Serve on buttered toast and with bacon. Decorate with tomato slices.